Nostalgic Memories
of
BRADFORD

2

The publishers would like to thank the following companies for their

support in the production of this book

Main sponsor
Aagrah Restaurants

ACW Garden Centre

Allan Jefferies

Astonish

Bradford Grammar School

Joseph H Clissold

Crossley Evans

Flexitallic

Joseph A. Hey & Son Ltd

Holmes, Mann & Co Ltd

Kashmir Crown Bakery

Kirkgate Centre

Provident Finance

Rex Procter & Partners

Sovereign Health Care

Shipley Transport Services

Thermocable (Flexible Elements) Ltd

Trevor Iles Ltd

Whaleys (Bradford) Ltd

Wright & Sons Ltd

Yorkshire Building Society

First published in Great Britain by True North Books Limited
England HX3 6SN
01422 244555
www.truenorthbooks.com

ISBN 978 - 1906649791

Text, design and origination by True North Books

Nostalgic Memories
of
BRADFORD

CONTENTS

INTRODUCTION

Such has been the popularity of our previous book on the Bradford area, that we have been encouraged to produce a new publication. Our books allow readers to walk on cobbled streets, browse in well known local shops of the period and revisit special events and occasions, without leaving the comfort of their favourite armchair.

'Change' is relentless and in some parts of the area the transformation will be more obvious than others. Bradford city centre and the roads around it have changed significantly from times gone by. Some of the older and architecturally impressive buildings have retained their originality on the outside, but their uses have changed.

The title of this new book, 'Nostalgic Memories of Bradford', tells you all you need to know about what is captured within its pages. Turning over leaf after leaf will bring you to a treasure trove from the last century. Through the photographs and thoughtful text, the reader is taken on a ride back through the mists of time to an age when mum would nip into Woolworths and dad could buy a suit at the Fifty Shilling Tailor. We make no apologies for the fact that some of the photographs will be outside living memory because they will still be familiar to us. They may feature an event described to us by a close relative or they could feature historical landmarks such as bridges and buildings.

Whatever the view taken on the boundaries which separate 'history', 'nostalgia' or 'the present', we should all invest a little time occasionally to reflect on the past and the people and events which helped to shape life as we know it today.

Bradford has always been a vibrant city, buzzing with energy, but different episodes in its life can be seen here. So, think of youthful days at the dance hall or courting in the cinemas of old and be entertained again as we revive Nostalgic Memories of Bradford…Happy memories!

TEXT	ANDREW MITCHELL, STEVE AINSWORTH, TONY LAX
PHOTOGRAPH RESEARCH	TONY LAX
DESIGNER	SEAMUS MOLLOY
BUSINESS DEVELOPMENT MANAGER	PETER PREST

VICTORIAN & EDWARDIAN
BRADFORD

Below and right: Pickard's brush manufacturing company had a shop on the corner of Kirkgate and Darley Street. Above it was a room for ladies to dine in some seclusion as there was a restaurant here, fitting in between Pickard's and the optician's beyond. There was still a strong element of sex segregation, especially among the middle and upper classes, in many areas of public activity in Edwardian Britain. Perhaps the small carriage on the left was waiting to collect a diner and take her back home for a restful afternoon with her embroidery. In the other image, also dating from 1904, Market Street was awash with shoppers without the worry of motorised transport confronting them as they crossed the street from Bowcliffe's shop or the Brown Muff department store, by the corner of Ivegate, on the left. They headed for WH Durans, an insurance broker, or the coal merchant near the junction with Bridge Street. At this corner an advert for Cambrian Railways recommended holidays in and around Cardigan Bay. Heading off to Wales was the equivalent of a continental holiday to our great grandparents. Some of the street furniture is delightfully period. especially Tte gas lamps on the corner.

Below: Horses and carts or carriages provided the transport along the expanse of Market Street on this late Victorian day. A liveried coachman waited patiently for his mistress to appear laden with fine hats in boxes or the best in silks and furs. Over the way, clerks and scribes in their natty business suits and bowler hats made their way to their offices. Out on the street, a cart laden with bales of wool looked to be on its way towards Cheapside. It was this commodity that had provided the basis for the production of worsted in large quantities from the start of the 1800s and on throughout the Industrial Revolution that turned a rural market town into a major manufacturing centre.

Above: The Bradford Exhibition of 1904 was held to emphasise the inauguration of Cartwright Hall in Manningham (Lister) Park. Displays of local textiles and engineering were mounted and a concert hall erected to show off the musical talents of the city's sons and daughters. Advances in medical treatment were advertised and a naval display was undertaken on the lake. The city streets were festooned with garlands and streamers in honour of both the occasion and that of Bradford's royal visitors. The ceremonial opening of the Exhibition was performed by The Prince and Princess of Wales, the future King George V and Queen Mary, on 4 May. They were staying at Harewood House and travelled in from Arthington by train. Their route from the city centre to Lister Park was lined by huge crowds.

Top right: Trams had a good safety record, but this one had bucked the odds and come to grief on Church Bank in July 1907. The photograph, as well as depicting the wreckage of the tramcar, gives an insight into human nature.

What is it about near disasters and accidents that prompt people to have a good nosey at the aftermath? You only have to drive past a motorway accident today to see scores of motorists slowing down to get a better look at someone else's misfortune. Here, a passer by examines the wreckage. What does he hope to find? Ghoulish.

> ## Did you know?
>
> *The name Bradford is derived from the Old English brad and ford (the broad ford) which referred to a crossing of the Bradford Beck at Church Bank below the site of Bradford Cathedral.*

Right: The tram heading towards us on Tyrrel Street in 1910 would shortly be passing the West Riding Window Cleaning Company and Staffordshire House on the left. The advert on the front of the tram was for Tit Bits, a weekly

magazine founded in 1881. It concentrated on human interest stories that had a sensationalist element, appealing to those who liked to be mildly shocked. In 1900, P G Wodehouse contributed an article 'Men who missed their own wedding'. The publication only ran out of steam in 1984. The image was captured as the Edwardian era drew to a close. Cars on the streets were becoming more frequent and the pace of life was increasing.

Above: The Norman Arch stands at one of the entrances to Lister Park. Situated at the end of the eastern promenade, it now defines the start of the Manningham conservation area. More plainly known as the Keighley Road Memorial Gatehouse, it was erected in 1882 to mark the visit of the Prince of Wales and his consort to the town. Its gothic style provides a handsome and striking opening into the parkland beyond. The castellated octagonal turrets quite openly state their grandeur. The arch's façade includes shield shaped tablets and alternate carvings of the white rose of Yorkshire and the feather motif of the Prince. The scene is dated to about 1900.

Bottom left and below: Over a century has passed since these scenes caught the cameraman's eye. It was in the opening years of the 20th century that we moved from Victorian times into the Edwardian era. The latter was shortlived, but it offered an opening to the changes that were to unfold in those days when peace and tranquility lived uncomfortably alongside social and economic turmoil and unrest. You would not have known that people were on the march for better conditions in the workplace or that women were mobilising their efforts to get parity in the electoral booths. Sitting on a bench in Peel Park, looking across at the fountain in the centre of the lake, meant that the cares of the world were miles away. This was our first public park, created as a memorial to Sir Robert Peel, the former Prime Minister and inspiration behind the formation of the modern police force. A mixture of public subscription and donations from local philanthropists provided the wherewithal and the park opened in 1853, three year's after Peel's death. The boating lake at Lister Park was a hit with visitors right from the start, offering opportunities to row its full length of some 100 yards or just simply stroll around its perimeter and feed the swans and ducks that had made this spot their home.

Below: In 1896 an Act of Parliament removed the prohibition on local authorities operating their own tramways and Bradford Council decided to construct and operate its own electric tramway. On 30 July, 1898, an electrified line was opened to Bolton Junction and a month later a further line to Great Horton came into service. Further tracks were laid in preparation for the large-scale expansion of the tramway. On 31 January, 1902, the horse trams that had been running on the Manningham Lane service since 1882 were finally retired as the system became fully operational. This photograph is thought to relate to the launch of the open top tram service in 1902. This very official looking group of men (most with moustaches), pose for the picture with special car No 118, a double deck 4-wheel, with a Peckham B9 truck, and a Brush body. This appears to be on of the inaugural trips to promote the new service. The picture was probably staged as the tram completed its journey at Saltaire. Later, Bradford Corporation Tramways built a tram shed to the west of the village, at the junction of Bingley Road and Saltaire Road. If you want to get a glimpse of Edwardian life at the start of the twentieth century, have a look at Mitchell and Kenyon's fantastic short film 'Electric tram rides from Forster Square, Bradford (1902).

Forster Square was once a vibrant part of the city centre through which traffic flowed and pedestrians strolled happily. The electric trams, as evidenced in the 1904 scene, soon proved popular after their introduction just a year or two earlier. Before then, it was a case of use your own legs or those of horses to help you get around. In the 1890s, the statue to the humanitarian Richard Oastler stood proudly looking across the square. He was a keen supporter of the rights of working children in mid 19th century Britain. He now stands on Northgate. By the latter years of the first decade of this century Forster Square looked like a wasteland, awaiting redevelopment as part of the Broadway project.

STREET SCENES

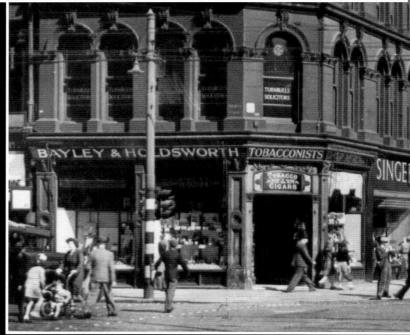

Market Street was always a busy part of town. In the picture taken on the eve of the outbreak of World War I we can see how quickly the motor car had developed as a major feature on our roads. Hardly a single one would have been spotted a dozen years earlier, but now they were already starting to clog the streets. By the 1950s they were bumper to bumper along the thoroughfare. In the later photo, looking from Bridge Street, the Singer building to the left is still there, though that name and such as Bayley and Holdsworth are not here any more. Brown Muff, further down Market Street, was a popular store, but it was sold in 1977 and became Rackham's in a takeover by the House of Fraser group. The store had its origins in the drapery opened by Henry Brown and his brother in law near to here in the mid

19th century. They moved to this Brown Muff building in 1870. The amusingly named 'Ann Teake's store', on the corner across from the tobacconist, has gone. A more modern structure currently occupies this spot facing what is now Centenary Square. It was home to the Lord Clarke pub for some years before it ran into difficulties in 2010. A year on, it was renamed the Ginger Goose. The Market Street section of Barclays became The Old Bank pub after the financiers left.

Did you know?

Bradford has more than 500,000 residents – the fourth largest metropolitan district in England. A total of 22.5 per cent of the population are under 16, compared with 19 per cent nationally.

Above: In 1927, Manningham Lane was a much quieter place than it is over three-quarters of a century later. Trying to weave a path through the traffic with which we now contend was not a problem for the tram making its way to Heaton. The destination village was once home to the author J B Priestley. In a flight of fancy we can imagine him revising the text of his earliest work, 'Adam in Moonshine, published this very year. Peter Sutcliffe, the 'Yorkshire Ripper', was a less wholesome former Heaton resident. The Bishop of Bradford is a more acceptable person who has his official home here. Heaton is one of the few places in the country that can still boast a Lord of the Manor.

Below: There was enough free fertiliser deposited on Shipley's Carr Lane to keep any number of rhubarb and rose growers happy. Children gathering on the street corner with Shaftesbury Avenue might spell hooliganism in the present day, but at the turn into the 20th century it simply meant that they were getting ready for a game. It might have been skipping, hopscotch, whip and top or British Bulldog. Whatever it was, it would have been harmless fun and no cause for alarm.

Below: It is hard to imagine from this quiet street scene that it would later make Saltaire a magnet for tourism in Bradford. Here was where Titus Salt and the River Aire came together to create the Victorian model villiage of Saltaire, in 1851. Victoria Road is the main thoroughfare through Saltaire, north to south. Looking north from the railway bridge, you can see on the right the administrative block of Salts Mill. On the left is Saltaire Dining Hall, which today is the Mill Building of Shipley College. This photo gives a good idea of why Sir Titus Salt relocated his entire business from the overcrowded and insanitary city of Bradford to this greenfield site, where he built his huge mill and the surrounding workers' village. The fields and moors of Shipley Glen and Baildon still offer a lovely countryside view. Sir Titus Salt gradually bought up parcels of land so that, at one time, most of what you can see belonged to him. In December 2001, Saltaire was designated a World Heritage Site by UNESCO. This means that the government has a duty to protect it.

This lovely view to the east across Forster Square take us back to when we were first getting used to being carried around on motorised transport, whether that be powered by electricity or petrol. The sharp eyed might be able to spot an ice cream seller in the top left of the square.

He was near the junction with Bolton Road, running away north, with Lower Kirkgate leading out centre left. The number of tram shelters dotted around the central area reminds us of how important this modern form of public transport had quickly become.

The smoking chimneys in the background also indicate how much the mills and the textile industry meant to the city economy in those days. There may have been fumes and filth in the air but never more was the saying about muck and brass more appropriate. The main building in view belonged to the General Post Office (GPO). Built in 1887, it is now known as St Peter's House, a centre for learning. Bradford Dyers Association, now Pennine House, was to the right on Church Bank, and Cathedral Close is to the left. The Cathedral's tower peeks above the old GPO.

Above: Extending from Rawson Square across to Market Street, Darley Street takes us through the heartland of the modern pedestrianised shopping experience. All the big names are here, competing merrily with some more interesting independent outlets. There were even more varied shops in 1943, even if the goods they sold were heavily restricted by wartime rationing. It seems as if one driver at least had been able to get some form of petrol allowance. Coupons were needed initially for the private motorist to travel modest distances, but these were scrapped in 1942. After then only official travel or essential users could get fuel. There was always the black market, but penalties were severe for those flouting regulations.

Did you know?

A mural on the back of the Priestley Centre For The Arts (visible from Leeds Road) commemorates the centenary of the founding of the Independent Labour Party in 1893.

Bottom left: The statue of Sir Robert Peel stood on Leeds Road looking across the square that was named for him. In 1851, his was the first public statue erected in Bradford. Although a prominent politician and reformer, there were some comments made about such an honour being bestowed on a Lancashire lad. Sculpted by William Behnes, the statue was cast in lead by Robinson Scott. When Kassapian's warehouse was demolished in the mid-1920s, Peel's grand figure was moved to the park in Undercliffe named after him. The dress of the young men in the foreground is interesting. They were clad in suits and waistcoats underneath their traditional flat caps.

Below: The 1920s were difficult times. The economy was in ruins after a world war that was financially crippling and also cost the nation the flowers of its youth, left behind in the poppy fields of Flanders. Companies such as the British Shoe Company, to the right, and Millett's on the other side of Westgate, to where Lingard's would transfer its business later, felt the pinch. Although Lloyd George, from his privileged perch at 10 Downing Street, promised much for those who had done their duty at home and abroad, the reality was continuing poor conditions, pay restraints and increasing unemployment. What price victory?

Above: Looking west, we have the Tyrrel Street and Sunbridge Road junction, along with Market Street. The vista dates from between the wars when the Saxone Shoe Company had just moved from a position on the other corner of Market Street. To the right is the Prudential building, designed by Alfred Waterhouse. It was built on Sunbridge Road in 1895 and is the only red brick and terracotta edifice of major importance to appear in the city. The District Bank, later the NatWest, designed by Milnes and France, appeared earlier on Market Street in 1873. To the left, the Mechanics institute, founded in 1832, played a leading role in adult education. Despite being a listed building, it fell foul of the developers in the mid-1970s. The library contents were rehoused on Kirkgate.

Left: Thought to date from May 1939, just a few months before the outbreak of war, this array of old posters on the bus garage wall contains some you might think would evoke a nostalgic thought or two. Yet, products such as Bovril, Gilbey's gin, Shippam's paste, Crosse and Blackwell's cans, Yardley's fragrance, Oxo cubes, Kilkof lozenges and Cephos headache powders are still with us or are recent enough for easy recall. Here no more, though, are George Robey, 'the prime minister of mirth', and Violet Lorraine who duetted with him on the pop standard 'If you were the only girl in the world'. They were topping the bill at the same time as Will Hay was starring in a movie at the new Ritz cinema.

Left: The Kirkgate shopping experience is now a mixture of retail outlets opening onto a pedestrianised way or a mall containing a variety of well known names. The days when lines of motor cars moved along its cobbled surface outside the Osborne Hotel or Melia's food distribution centre have long been consigned to history. To the left, Ronsmans was a top-class establishment that provided the best in furs, gowns, coats and costumes. However, there is no more singing to be heard from Novello's or anywhere else. Such is progress.

Left: If you want a little bit of inspirational floristy, that can now be found at the Greenhouse shop where Lloyds Bank used to be on the corner of what is still a cobbled Hampton Place and High Street, in Idle. There is nowhere for the men to sit these days and the bridge has also gone. There is now a branch of the Yorkshire Bank to the right, where High Street levels out. What was once the village green is just out of shot, to the right before the shops. The photographer was standing near the White Swan pub at the junction with Albion Road and Bradford Road.

Below: Just to our left, slightly out of shot, stands the stature of the old queen who once lent her name to this spot. Known well into the last century as Victoria Square at the junction between Little Horton Lane and Godwin Street, this section of the city is still intact. The statue was unveiled in 1904 and the war memorial in the centre of the image was erected in 1922. Designed by city architect Walter Williamson, it was unveiled on the sixth anniversary of the start of the Battle of the Somme where so many members of the Bradford Pals' Regiment perished. To the left, the New Victoria was built on the site of Whittaker's brewery and opened in 1930 as a vast ciné-theatre catering for 3,300 customers. It became the Gaumont in 1950 just after this photograph was taken. The movie showing then was 'The Eagle and the Hawk', starring John Payne, Dennis O'Keefe and the much married Rhonda Fleming. A change of cinema name to the Odeon occurred in 1969, before closing in 2000.

Did you know?

The National Media Museum (previously the National Museum of Photography, Film & Television) celebrates cinema and movies, and is the most visited museum outside London. It contains an Imax cinema and was once described by David Puttnam as the best cinema in Britain.

Forster Square, as seen in 1952 (right), had changed little since the time around the First World War that is illustrated in the other two images. It was only in the final quarter of the last century that its face was to change more dramatically. Socially and economically, there were some similarities in that the later view occurred during an austere period in Britain. In the 1950s we had to come to terms with not being the main player on the world stage any more as we were heavily in debt to the Americans. Even just before the First World War we started to feel the effects of falling trade and the reliance on overseas markets. This became much more obvious in time as our problems were exacerbated by the Wall Street crash at the end of the 1920s. There was no obvious effect on Forster Square. John Birnie Philip's statue of Richard Oastler, flanked by two children in working clothes, was here until the 1960s before being relocated at Rawson Square and then on Northgate. In the meantime, the humanitarian's memorial garden continued to flourish and provide a quiet haven for locals to have a breather from the daily routine shopping or working in the nearby railway offices. The Hotel Metropole, on the right in the above view, was to become a YMCA centre in 1916. It is no longer there, but on a happier note we still have the Midland Hotel and some of the other attractive structures around Lower Kirkgate and Cheapside.

Above: Perched high on a hill overlooking Bradford one way and Halifax the other, Queensbury is a place with its own identity. Once named Queenshead after the packhorse pub here, the village takes particular pride in being home to the Black Dyke Mills and its internationally renowned brass band. Standing on the top of Holy Trinity Church, the photographer was looking northeast along Chapel Street and High Street towards Clayton. The bus turning out of Granby Street was alongside the memorial cross, unveiled on 2 September, 1922, as a mark of respect to those who fell in World War I. Further names were added on 14 May, 1950, to include those lost in World War II.

Bottom left: Southern softies think that all northern towns and cities are full of grime and flat caps. Well, think again. From Bradford, we are just a few miles from the hills, moors and dales that are idyllic parts of Yorkshire. Looking down the A658 Harrogate Road towards Apperley Bridge, this is still a pleasant view today. The trees may be leafier and more buildings lining parts of the road, but there yet remains something of a panorama towards Pool and Harewood beyond. In the immediate distance we can spot Woodhouse Grove School. This opened in 1812 as a preparatory boarding school for the sons of Methodist ministers. It is now a secondary school and sixth form college and the campus includes the nearby Bronte House and Ashdown Lodge that cater for primary and nursery aged children, respectively. Former Test cricketer, the late Graham Roope, was once the school groundsman.

Did you know?

St George's Hall is a grand concert hall dating from 1853, making it the oldest concert hall in Britain and the third oldest in the whole of Europe.

Below: This parade of shops along High Street in Queensbury, does not look much different today, although the shop owners have changed. Back in the 1940s when this photograph was taken, this section of the High Street offered a range of shops and services that included Halifax Building Society, Crocketts Cleaners, Carter's grocery shop and Stocks stores. We can also see the two Co-op buildings near the end of Chapel Street. The Co-op still have a presence with a single storey building just further round to the left. Behind the Ford van, we can see a small child in a white pram outside the shop. How many mums today, would feel comfortable leaving their child unattended in this way? Not many suspect, but in those days they would not think twice about it. Whichever era you are talking about, Queensbury has always had that special village feel.

Martins dry cleaning business evolved from a company set up by the Johnson Brothers in Bootle in 1932 and, although the parent company has gone, the name is still in use in many towns today. The 1946 look down Ivegate (above) includes a traditional barber's pole with its red and white helical stripes indicating that simple surgery was also on offer from the barber in medieval times. Supposedly, the poor patient clung onto the pole in an attempt to dull the pain of bloodletting and the like. Another look at Ivegate in the 1950s (right) includes memories of Smith's stationery business and that of the butcher, J H Dewhurst. Just beyond the snack bar, there was an opportunity to sample a Melbourne ale or two in the Grosvenor. Despite its name, this was a beer brewed in Leeds. Its logo included a picture of a bowing courtier that can occasionally be seen on former Melbourne brewery pubs today. The Unicorn Hotel that closed in the 1980s belonged to the better known Tetley company. The lady in the window next to the Tetley sign (pictured top right) appears to be staring right at the photographer. What ever the reason, she doesn't look to be too happy about the situation. Coincidentally, Tetley's took Melbourne into its empire in 1960. Ivegate is now part of the pedestrianised heart of the centre, entered from Market Street through a wrought iron arch erected in 1988.

In this set of pictures there is an image of life in Town Hall Square taken in 1904, while the accompanying pair dates from nearly half a century later. The similarity in the settings is that all the photographs were taken from approximately the same position on the square, looking northeast. Many of the shops that we can see were cleared as this area was redeveloped as City and then Centenary Square. In the earlier times depicted here we can hark back to the days when Tyrell Street ran away to the left of Burton's, with its 'Dress You' exhortation on the building façade. Market Street was to its right, separating 'the tailor of taste' from the Town Hall. The buses in one shot include FKY 1 that was on the 749 route to Buttershaw, a postwar housing development composed of a high percentage of council property. Halford's Corner, as some referred to it, was on the left from where Thornton Road heads out west for several miles until it meets the A629 Halifax-Keighley Road. Those with long memories will recall Tyrell Street's Collinson's Café. The aroma of fresh coffee and the tuneful airs played by Bradford's style of Palm Court trio, led by Arthur Clarke, marked this establishment as the place to be mid-morning or for afternoon tea. In its heyday, Collinson's employed 40 staff, but changing tastes led to its closure in 1969. Next door was the more mundane Farmer Giles Milk Bar. The Edwardian picture shows the building opposite the Town Hall when Meshe Osinsky was still being transformed into Montague Burton over in Chesterfield.

Did you know?

The Bradford Mela, the biggest of its kind outside Asia, takes place in June. The word mela is Sanskrit for 'a gathering' or 'to meet'.

Above: Manningham, situated about a mile north of the city centre, is now seen as the centre of the local south Asian population. In earlier times, it was a mixture of splendid villas and large houses that existed in close proximity to rows of back-to-back terraced properties. Many of these provided accommodation for millworkers and management who lived close to one another but very much apart in their styles of abode. One of the most memorable of the buildings on Manningham Lane belonged to Busby's. You could shop until you dropped in a department store that seemed to have everything.

Top right: The 1937 aerial view that includes the old Christ Church to the right and takes in Hallfield Road, Eldon Place and Drewton Road, is dominated by the magnificent building on Manningham Lane. This was Busby's department store, one of the most prestigious in the north of England. It offered much more than just clothing, furniture and everyday items. It was

the establishment where those with discerning tastes could select from the finest wares and enjoy being pampered in its salons. Advertising itself as 'the store with the friendly welcome', it was founded by Ernest W Busby in 1908 when he moved his business from the Royal Arcade. In its later years the store was taken over by Debenhams, but sadly lost business and closed in 1978 and was destroyed by fire a year later.

Right: Tyrell Street was once a busy thoroughfare with both motor and trolley buses heading out towards St Luke's Hospital, Canterbury Avenue and Little Horton on the 61 and 47 routes. In more modern times part of the southern end has gone and much of the remainder pedestrianised. It is a change from this early post-war scene when we were trying to make our way back to prosperity during the era known as 'austerity Britain'. As the 1950s headed towards closure, Prime Minister Macmillan was able to claim that 'we had never had it so good'.

Above: In the 1960s, some of the properties in sight were already boarded up in preparation for redevelopment of this part of the city that saw the old John Street market disappear. The Rawson Hotel, on the corner with Rawson Place, dated from 1899, and provided one end of the frontage to the market. It has an impressive colonnaded corner turret and dome and is about all that is left of that once imposing façade. Designed by Hope and Jondine, architects from the technical college, the hotel became a Grade II listed building in August 1983.

Bottom left: A late afternoon view of Town Hall Square from Thornton Road in 1954. On the right is the Town Hall in all its Gothic splendour, which was designed by Lockwood and Mawson and completed in 1873, at a cost of £100,000. This is a unique view of Town Hall Square and gives a splendid impression of what the centre of Bradford looked like on an ordinary working day around sixty years ago. We can see the trolleybus rounding the Square, interestingly followed by a British Railways delivery vehicle. How many reader have been caught short and needed to spend a penny in the Crystal Palace toilets, in the forefront of this picture. The facility boasted an attendant who would make sure everything was clean and tidy in the cubicles. The cleanliness of this establishment was commendable and would be envied today. Unfortunately, there is no chance of relief today as the toilets were filled in and this area was developed and pedestrianised in 1997, as part of the city's Centenary Square.

Did you know?

Among the rulers whose sculpted likenesses adorn City Hall is Oliver Cromwell, who, of course, was never crowned King.

Below: Despite being able to identify Church Bank on the far side of the building with the Players Please slogan on its top floor, this spot between Bolton Road and Canal Road, near Lower Kirkgate, is hard to recognise now. In fact, it is well nigh impossible as Forster Square has altered so dramatically since the 1950s. Topham and Mortimer, names on the shops to the left, are but distant memories. The square was named after philanthropist William E Forster who served us a local MP for quarter of a century from 1861.

The changing face of Bradford in the mid-60s is recorded for us in this photograph from the time. On one side of Broadway, British Home Stores is not yet ready for opening, and the hoardings are still up. Young's jewellers, Burtons, Hardy's and other businesses, however, are already up and running in the new building. Central House blocks the view towards Hall Ings and further to the left we can see the Bradford Dyers Association Ltd building (Pennine House). No such problem with the view today, as we would be looking out over a massive derelict blot on the landscape. How strange it seems now to see traffic passing along Broadway, which has been a pedestrian only area for many years. This spot, viewed from the Midland Hotel, was to see the extending of Cheapside and the building of Petergate on the far side of the new buildings. The two main thoroughfares would meet at a large roundabout in Forster Square.

In the 1950s and 1960s, much of central Bradford was redeveloped to the design of Stanley Wardley. This included a new main road, Petergate, linking a completely remodelled Forster Square to Leeds Road at Eastbrook Well roundabout. Part of the gardens remained as a walled enclave in a busy traffic roundabout, accessible to pedestrians only by underpasses. Two large modern buildings were built on the west side: Central House and Forster House, a John Poulson design. Apart from the station, the only building fronting the square that survived redevelopment was St Peter's House, which was for a long time the central post office for Bradford. Here we can see the city centre above Leeds Road in 1962. Eastbrook Well is almost complete and the Wolfe and Hollander 'tower' is finished with the rooftop car park already in use. It is sadly a much different picture today, with much of this area raised to the ground and empty open areas of derelict land in its place.

One of the many changes to Bradford's profile is taking shape in the picture left. A multi-storey car park, one of a number, makes its entry onto the scene, along with the rooftop car park at the C&A building by the Eastbrook Well-Petergate roundabout. The twin arches of the Exchange Railway Station, having survived for nearly a century, were demolished in 1976. The new Law Courts were also established on Drake Street as part of the redevelopment phase about 1990. The vacant plot towards the centre of the picture was to become Norfolk Gardens, with its fountain and city centre version of a large paddling pool.

t would seem that any view across Forster Square taken in the last half century would show one of change in the making. Some might comment that it seldom seems as if it is ever in the completion stages. Towards the top left, the domed building housed a department for British Railway Goods Services. Behind

it, lies Forster Square Station. Its origins can be found in 1890, when a third incarnation of stations was unveiled. The roofing was replaced in the 1960s at a time when some people referred to it as Market Street Station. However, that name did not stick. A new station was built in 1990, a little to the west of the one we can see.

Aagrah Restaurants
The Taste of Kashmir

When it comes to Asian cuisine one name that stands out from all the rest in Bradford is the Aagrah Group of Restaurants, which has been creating history for over three decades.

Mohammed Sabir MBE, Hons Dbs opened his first restaurant in Shipley in 1977 with the aim of presenting authentic Kashmiri cuisine of the highest order to the people of Shipley and Bradford. Aagrah has since expanded and created a niche amongst those appreciative of good authentic Asian food served in opulent surroundings.

This family-run restaurant group has prospered and grown over the years in response to the local and regional community acknowledging the standards set by Aagrah. The special

qualities first created in Shipley have since been recreated successfully with branches of the Aagrah restaurant now throughout the Yorkshire region and beyond.

With family members personally managing each restaurant they follow an ethos of combining authentic dishes, as prepared in the Kashmiri homeland, with the highest possible standard of food service. These personal touches and passion have brought the group national and international recognition over the years.

Above: Founder, Mohammed Sabir and his wife Fazilat. *Below:* Where it all began, Aagrah Westgate, as Mohammed Sabir is congratulated on receiving the first of many awards won by Aagrah Restaurants, 1978.

of the East India Company in 1608, and more permanently in 1612. As the influence of the British in India grew, so too did the interest in Indian food back in England, leading to the publishing of recipes and the commercial creation of curry powder in 1780.

The first appearance of curry on a restaurant menu was in 1773 at the Coffee House in Norris Street, Haymarket, London. The first establishment dedicated to Indian cuisine, however, was the Hindostanee Coffee House located at 34, George Street, Portman Square, London in 1809. It was opened by Dean Mahomet originally from Patna, Bihar, India. Dean Mahomet appreciated the interest in all things Indian and offered a house 'for the Nobility and Gentry where they might enjoy the Hookah and Indian dishes of the highest perfection'. Decor was very colonial, with bamboo chairs and picture-bedecked walls, and it proved to be very popular.

Innovation is another key to Aagrah's success, with new dishes being constantly introduced to the menus. The company is only too happy to share the secrets of the Aagrah chef with its customers, with many of the famous favourite recipes found in company recipe books that are available for sale.

Growing success in 2001 enabled the company to invest in the development of a purpose-built CPU (Central Production Unit) in Shipley. This enabled the group to cater with ease to small and large scale outdoor catering events throughout the UK.

Aagrah aims to continue developing in the future, providing its customers with a memorable dining experience with menu prices always at an economic and acceptable level. They are continuing to grow on the premise that they "Provide a variety of fresh, healthy and nutritious dishes at affordable prices in truly comfortable and relaxing surroundings, always to the total satisfaction of all valued customers".

The history of Indian food in Britain is four hundred years old. Apart from the reports of occasional explorers, the story really starts with the arrival in Surat in India of the English merchants

Unfortunately, outgoings were greater than incomings and Mahomet had to file for bankruptcy in 1812, although the restaurant carried on without him until 1833.

In the years since then Asian cuisine has proved to be increasingly popular in Britain, especially since the arrival in Britain of large numbers of experienced and able cooks in the 1950s and 1960s. One of those new pioneers was Mohammed Sabir, who hailed from Kashmir.

Top left: *Building the Pudsey branch in 1986.*
Left: *Mohammed Sabir and staff pictured in the new Pudsey premises in 1987.* **Above:** *Aagrah Pudsey receive the Restaurant of the Year award for 1989.*

Kashmir, noted for the beauty of its scenery, is the northwestern region of the Indian subcontinent. Until the mid-19th century, the term Kashmir geographically denoted only the valley between the Great Himalayas and the Pir Panjal mountain range. Today Kashmir denotes a larger area that includes the Indian-administered state of Jammu and Kashmir (which consists of the divisions: the Kashmir valley, Jammu and Ladakh), the Pakistani-administered Gilgit–Baltistan and the Azad Kashmir provinces, and the Chinese-administered regions of Aksai Chin and Trans-Karakoram Tract.

The area is not only noted for its mountains and lakes, but also for its fine food. Rogan josh for example is undoubtedly considered the most emblematic version of all Kashmiri curry dishes. Rogan josh (or roghan josh) is an aromatic lamb dish, which is one of the signature recipes of Kashmiri cuisine.

It was from this spectacular region with its fabulous gastronomic heritage that Mohammed Sabir arrived in the city of Bradford in the 1960s, where he worked first in the textile mills and then as a bus driver.

Yet, in 1976 things changed for Mohammed. That year, aged 38, he bought a mobile takeaway van known as Spice Pot from which he and his wife, Fazilat Sabir, began selling their unique brand of Kashmiri food. The following year a proper restaurant opened at 27 Westgate, Shipley; it would remain the Aagrah base for the next 24 years until moving to 4, Saltaire Road, Shipley in 2001.

Joined by the founder's two brothers, Mohammed Aslam MBE and Zafar Iqbal, the Aagrah team would in due course expand the business to a degree not even dreamt of back in 1977. Since 1977, under the guidance of Sabir, the family-led Aagrah group has opened a further 14 restaurants in Yorkshire, including five in Leeds.

Top left: The Emmerdale cast enjoy a vist to Aagrah in 1988.
Left and below: Aagrah Tadcaster (left) which opened in 1996, and the re-opening of Aagrah Westgate in 2002 (below). *Above:* Brothers, Mohammed Sabir (centre), Mohammed Aslam (left), and Zafar Iqbal.

Rogan means 'oil' in Persian, while josh means 'heat, hot, boiling, or passionate'. Rogan josh thus means cooked in oil at intense heat. Another interpretation of the name rogan josh is derived from the word rogan meaning 'red colour' (the same Indo-European root that is the source of the French 'rouge'" and the Spanish 'rojo') and josh meaning passion or heat. Rogan josh was brought to Kashmir by the Mughals, whose cuisine was in turn influenced by Persian cuisine. The unrelenting summer heat of the Indian plains took the Mughals frequently to Kashmir, which has a cooler climate because of its high altitude.

Moving onwards, and in the continued direction of success that the chain has achieved since it began, their extensive plans to expand and progress the company was demonstrated in 2009 with the opening of The Midpoint Suite, a huge banqueting centre in Pudsey catering for private and corporate functions.

The most recent branch has now opened in Bristol. The restaurant chain's success has been recognised by among others the British Curry Awards, which named it 'Best Restaurant'. The group is also listed in some of the country's top restaurant guides and by the Michelin Guide, which features all Aagrah restaurants.

International Trust, whose annual charity dinners raise large amounts of money for good causes, UK charities as well as abroad, not least the victims of the Pacific Tsunami and the Pakistan earthquakes.

As a result of Mohammed Sabir's tireless charity work he was awarded an MBE in the Queen's 2006 New Year's Honours list, as well as a Lifetime Achievement Award from the Bradford Community Awards in the same year. Bradford Council's acting chief executive David Kennedy summed up the sentiment when he hailed award winners and nominees as "positive role models for us all to follow."

*Above: Mohammed Aslam at work. **Left:** The International Indian Chef of the Year certificate awarded to Mohammed Aslam for 1995/96. **Below:** Mr and Mrs Mohammed Sabir pictured at Leeds Met University after Mr Sabir received his Honorary Doctorate.*

INTERNATIONAL INDIAN CHEF OF THE YEAR COMPETITION

Bengal Tiger House, 91 Henderson Street, Leith, Edinburgh, EH6 6ED
Telephone: 0131 553 3980 · Fax: 0131 313 1398

This is to certify that

...... *Mr Mohammed Aslam* ......

*was the winner
in the*
*International Indian Chef of the Year Competition
1995/96*

**TOMMY MIAH
EVENTS ORGANISER**

PANEL OF JUDGES				EXPERT ADVISORS	
Ms Lisa Aziz, Sky News	Mr Malcolm Dunbar, Sales Director, Moet & Chandon	Mr Allan Hill, Executive Chef, Gleneagles Hotel	Mr Ralph Porciani, Executive Chef, Regents Hotel, London	Tommy Miah, Executive Chef of the Raj Restaurant	Mrs Khan Panni, Finalist, Indian Chef of the Year 91/92
Ms Audrey Baxter, Managing Director, W.A. Baxter & Son Ltd.	Mr Michael Edwards, Vice-President, American Express Travel	Ms Catey Hillier, Editor, Caterer and Hotel Keeper Chef	Mr Ian Rushbrook, Director, Rushbrook Investments	Mrs Khan, Executive Chef of Moet & Chandon	Matab Miah, Chef & Managing Director of Vojon Restaurant in Newcastle
Mr Anis Choudhury, Tommy Miah's Curry Club	Sir Alistair Grant, Chairman, Argyll Group Plc	Mr Prem Kumar, Executive Chef, Dubai Golf & Racing Club	Mr Colin Shepherd M.P., Chairman, (House of Commons Catering Select Committee)	Mr Gordon Watt, Moet & Chandon	Mr Azam Khan, Finalist, Indian Chef of the Year 92/93
Ms Jackie Clemson, Selector - Indian Dishes, Marks & Spencer Plc.	Mr Paul Griffiths, Director of Provisions, ASDA	Sir Ian Maclaurin, Chairman, Tesco Plc.	Mr Richard Shepherd, (Chairman of Panel of Judges) Langan's Brasserie, London	Mr Abdul Malik, Star of India Restaurant, Cheam, Surrey	
Lord Meghnad Desai, London School of Economics	Mr Kurt Haffner, Head of Culinary Concepts, British Airways		Ms Meena Patak, Director, Patak Spices Ltd.	Ms Mitzie Wilson, Editor BBC Good Food Magazine	

Indian Chef of the Year Competition is a division of Tommy Miah's Curry Club
Registered in Scotland No. 120392 Registered Office: 91 Henderson Street, Edinburgh

It is no surprise to discover that Mohamed Aslam won the coveted accolade as International Indian Chef of the Year 1995/96.

Public recognition has, however, gone even further.

Mohammed Sabir has helped to raise over £1.5 million for charities in England and Pakistan and, in 2002, he set up the charitable arm of the Aagrah group, the Jannat Welfare

It was the death in 1983 of Mr Sabir's son, nine-year-old Sajid, which prompted him to begin raising cash for charity. Bolling Special School, where Sajid had been a pupil, has been one of the causes to benefit. As Mr Sabir explained "All my charity work stems from the death of my disabled son Sajid who was born with cerebral palsy. After his death at just nine and a half years old I felt an urge to do what I could in terms of helping people, especially at Bolling Special School in Bradford where he had been treated so well".

Mr Sabir was in the Pakistani area of Mirpur when the South Asian earthquake struck in October 2005, and stayed on in the region for more than two months administering help through funds raised here. He leapt into action to co-ordinate fundraising efforts of people across the district, and then personally delivered aid to people in the devastated region.

Within two days of the earthquake, staff working in his ten Aagrah restaurants had raised more than £30,000 to help people in the immediate aftermath.

Mr Sabir said of his MBE: "It's a great honour and I'm very proud and happy. The Aagrah group raises over £100,000 for charity every year. I'd like to say thank you to the people who put my name up for this."

Mohammed Aslam, Managing Director and Executive Chef of the Aagrah Group of Restaurant, has also since been honoured with an MBE in recognition for his services to the hospitality industry in the Queen's New Year's Honours List in January 2010.

Above left: *Mohammed Sabir handing over much needed medicinces to Prof Bushra Khar for Rawalpindi General Hospital following the earthquake in Pakistan.* ***Below and bottom:*** *Interior and exterior views of Aagrah's Saltaire Road, Shipley, premises.*

More personal accolades followed. The founder of Aagrah, the country's largest and most successful Kashmiri restaurant group, Mohammed Sabir MBE, was awarded an honorary degree by Leeds Metropolitan University as part of the Summer Graduation celebrations. The ceremony took place on Monday, 18 July, 2011, at the Headingley Campus.

Speaking after the ceremony Mohammed Sabir said: "It is a really proud day and a great honour to receive this honorary award from Leeds Metropolitan. I would encourage today's graduating students to use your education wisely, work hard and follow your dreams in all of your life."

Mohammed has certainly followed his own advice since opening his first restaurant in Shipley in 1977 with the aim of presenting authentic Kashmiri cuisine of the highest order to the people of Yorkshire and beyond. Aagrah has since expanded and created a niche amongst those appreciative of good authentic Asian food served in opulent surroundings. This family-run restaurant group has prospered and grown over the last 35 years in response to the local and regional community acknowledging the standards set by Aagrah. The special qualities created in Shipley have since been recreated successfully at all branches of the Aagrah restaurant chain.

Meanwhile, not all the group's growth has been in its restaurants. Aagrah has recreated the taste of its famous foods in a range of ready-made sauces which marked a move into retail manufacturing. The range of tarka cooking sauces was developed by Mohammed Aslam, managing director and executive chef, to replicate the taste of the group's restaurants at home. The 18 month long project would see the Aagrah sauces appear on the shelves of Asda and Tesco supermarkets throughout Yorkshire. However, producing sauces for home consumption does not mean that the restaurants are being forgotten; far from it. The long term plan is now to double the number of restaurants over the next ten years.

The Aagrah story, its growth from a single takeaway van to a national chain of restaurants, is an astonishing one - but no more remarkable than that of Mohammed Sabir and the family which has made it all possible.

Left: Guest of honour The Lord-Lieutenant of West Yorkshire, Dr Ingrid M Roscoe, pictured with Mohammed Sabir and Mohamed Aslam. Bottom left: Aagrah's range of Chutnies (left) and Tarka Cooking Sauces. Above and below: Exterior and interior views of The Midpoint Suite. For more information on The Midpoint Suite and Aagrah Restaurants visit www.aagrah.com

A s the guns roared over Flanders in the summer of 1915 and news reached us of bitter struggles at Gallipoli, some were able to ignore what was happening in those bloodbaths. Perhaps they were not yet aware of the real horrors being endured by friends and foes alike. The bandstand at Manningham Park, its surrounding grassed areas and stretch of promenade provided the chance to relax in the sunshine. Today, most of us know this idyllic part of the city as Lister Park. It bears the name of the 1st Earl of Masham, Samuel Cunliffe Lister, the industrialist who sold the land to the city at a knock-down price. The photographs were taken during the centenary of his birth.

Did you know?

Within the city district there are 37 parks and gardens. Lister Park, with its boating lake and Mughal Water Gardens, was voted Britain's Best Park for 2006.

ENTERTAINMENT, LEISURE & PASTIMES

S t. George's Hall was built in 1853, designed in a neo-classical style by the architects Lockwood & Mawson, who also designed Bradford City Hall, the Wool Exchange and the World Heritage Village Saltaire. The Hall was officially opened on 29 August, 1853, by HRH Queen Victoria and HRH Prince Albert. It is the oldest Concert Hall still in use in the UK and the third oldest in Europe. Although St George's Hall had been putting on film shows from as early as 1898, the Hall officially became a cinema in 1926 and was initially operated by New Century Pictures. On the 25 March, 1949, Bradford Council purchased the hall and started to modernise the venue so that it would be suitable for concerts, entertainments and public meetings. After more than four years in the making, the Hall was officially re-

This building boasts an amazing and colourful history, including being home to the longest running orchestral season in the UK, it is now in its 134th year with the Halle in their season as resident Orchestra. Over the years thousands of famous people have appeared here, from Charles Dickens in 1854, to Harry Houdini in 1905, and more recently a host of musical rock and pop legends which include, Deep Purple, Queen, David Bowie, Iron Maiden and Bon Jovi. It is home to a wide range of entertainment bringing the cream of touring music, comedy and variety to the region.

This photograph showing the main frontage, on Bridge Street, is from around 1939, at the time the main feature film 'I Stole A Million', starring George Raft and Claire

Above: The Saltaire Picture House enjoyed a prominent position at the busy junction of Bingley Road and Saltaire Road and opposite the former tram depot. Designed by a local Bradford architect and City Alderman, William Illingworth, it opened on 17 June, 1922, with the promise, of the 'most up to date pictures and best music'. One of the first films to show was 'The Fortune of Christina McNab', produced in 1921. It was later taken over by Denman Picture Houses Ltd and in 1941 was absorbed into the Gaumont British Picture Corporation, becoming the 'Gaumont' after the war in 1945. Local folk still tended to call it Saltaire Picture House, probably because the huge embossed stone name was an integral part of the frontage design. Less than a year after modernisation, the Gaumont suddenly closed on Saturday, 19 October, 1957. The last film to feature was 'Lust for Life' starring Kirk Douglas and Anthony Quinn. The building was eventually demolished in June 1966 and the site was cleared to make way for a garage and filling station.

Right: This is an unfamiliar picture to most of us, of the Empire Theatre at the rear of the Alexandra Hotel. Architect W J Sprague designed the Empire Music Hall, which was opened on the 30 January, 1899. Music hall acts that appeared at the Empire in the early years included such notable names as Stan Laurel, Charlie Chaplin on several occasions, Fred Karno, and W.C Fields. Even the great Harry Houdini performed at the Bradford Empire in 1911. As we can see in this photograph, the entrance to the theatre was via the wide steps to the pillared hotel entrance. From 1914, Francis Laidler's newly-built Alhambra Theatre, only a few yards away across the road, caused the Empire audiences to decline resulting in its closure as a variety theatre in April 1916. It did re-open later as the Theatre & Opera House, but this lasted for only fifteen months before a fire destroyed the stage. In February, 1918, the Empire re-opened as a cinema which ran successfully for many years. We can only guess what the sign on the adjacent building says. The fact that F. L. Harris offers high class, American painless extracts, perhaps we can assume it is...artificial teeth. We will leave you to make your own mind up.

Right: The 1910-11 season was to prove to be Bradford City's pinnacle, in 100 years of Football League membership. Jimmy Speirs scored 7 goals in his 25 League appearances and helped City to finish 5th, just seven points behind Champions Manchester United – their highest-ever finish in the Football League. However, even this was overshadowed by Bradford City's exploits in the FA Cup that season. The 1911 Final was the 40th FA Cup final and City went into the game as underdogs, against the cup holders, Newcastle United. The Final took place at the Crystal Palace on 22 April, 1911,

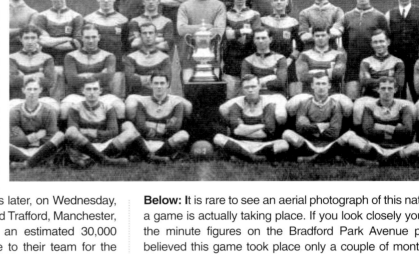

and ended in a goalless draw. Four days later, on Wednesday, 26 April, 1911, the replay took place at Old Trafford, Manchester, before an attendance of 66,646, with an estimated 30,000 locked out. Bradford made one change to their team for the replay with Bob Torrance coming in for Gildea, who never played for City again. History was made - Jimmy Speirs' headed goal won the cup for City, in only their eighth year in existence. An estimated 100,000 people welcomed the team back to Bradford outside the old Exchange Station and it took the entourage more than an hour to make the short journey to a Civic Reception at the Midland Hotel. It was a new trophy that Speirs lifted, appropriately made by Bradford jewellers Fattorini's. The cup triumph remains City's only major honour.

Below: It is rare to see an aerial photograph of this nature when a game is actually taking place. If you look closely you can see the minute figures on the Bradford Park Avenue pitch. It is believed this game took place only a couple of months before the World Cup Final in 1966. Cars can be seen parked around the ground at what is thought to be the last home game of the season, against Stockport County played on 25 May, 1966. At the time, Bradford were in the old Division 4 and finished in mid-table after winning the game 3-1. You can clearly see the fabulous cricket pavillion, the so called 'Dolls House' and the dual-sided grandstand, that was shared by both football and cricket spectators. There is also evidence in the bottom of this photograph, of the old Horton Park Railway Station. The station was closed in 1952, although the platforms had been kept intact for the occasional football specials. Adjacent to the cricket ground is one of Bradford's first supermarkets, operated by Wm Morrison. Financial problems brought about the sale of the ground in 1973.

Did you know?

Jimmy Speirs, who scored the winning goal for Bradford City FC in the 1911 FA cup final, was killed during the Battle of Passchendaele in 1917 during the First World War

In August 1928, Bradford City recorded their biggest home victory, when they beat Rotherham United 11-1.

Above: The 1950s brought a return of League derbies with Bradford (PA) following Avenue's relegation from Division Two in 1950. In terms of League standing Avenue fared better than City in the first half of the decade although without establishing themselves as serious promotion challengers. In the first derby of the 1950/51 season at Park Avenue on 30 September City were beaten 1-3 with the official attendance stated as 25,655 (the highest post-war derby crowd). In the return game of the 1950/51 season in February, 1951 18,454 watched City beat Avenue 4-1. Bradford wore their change shirt for this game which was the same design as that worn by Bradford Northern until fairly recently. Eddie Carr, who scored 56 goals for City in 99 League and Cup games between 1949-53, is seen beating the Bradford keeper to the ball and passing to Whelan (Polly) Ward who scored from close range. Carr and Greenhoff (2) scored the other City goals. Ward played 156 games for City and scored 42 goals. He left City in 1954 to join non-League King's Lynn but signed for Park Avenue the following year where he established himself as a popular goalscoring inside-forward.

Right: In 1966 there were two fairly significant changes to the ground. The open Bradford end terrace was finally covered and the club's former offices and dressing rooms at the bottom of Burlington Terrace (on the north west corner of

the kop) were demolished. The current office and dressing room complex at the corner of the main stand and Bradford end was constructed in 1961 and it is now the oldest surviving part of Valley Parade. A plan in 1963 to erect a glass fibre roof over the kop never got off the drawing board.

The aerial views of Odsal Stadium show just how basic the facilities once were for a vast crowd of spectators who flocked here from 1934 onwards. When first leased to Bradford Northern for use as a rugby league stadium, it was little more than a tip in an old quarry. Somehow, a stand, clubhouse and offices were built, terraces that were a mixture of concrete and open earthworks were created and a pitch laid. Despite the somewhat primitive conditions, crowds flocked to the ground, especially during the postwar years. In 1954, over 102,000 spectators watched the Challenge Cup replay played here between Warrington and Halifax. Over the years, the stadium has hosted other sports such as speedway, stock car racing, soccer and show jumping. The capacity since redevelopment is now a much more modest, but comfortable, 20,000.

Right: This was an early team photo of the rugby league side founded as Bradford Northern in 1907 when it split from Bradford Park Avenue with the latter side switching to play football. A rugby club bearing the city's name first appeared in 1863, playing at Horton Cricket Club for a while before adopting a nomadic life until settling at Park Avenue in 1879. Six years later it was one of the founder members of the Northern Rugby Football Union. After the parting of the ways with Bradford PA, the newly-named Northern played briefly at Dudley Hill before going to Birch Lane. The move to Odsal Top took place in 1934. When the summer era of rugby began in 1996, the club was renamed Bradford Bulls.

Darlinson, Greaves, Tyler, Foster and Traill. This game against near neighbours and rivals Halifax, was the first time a final at Wembley had sold out, with a record attendance of 95,050.

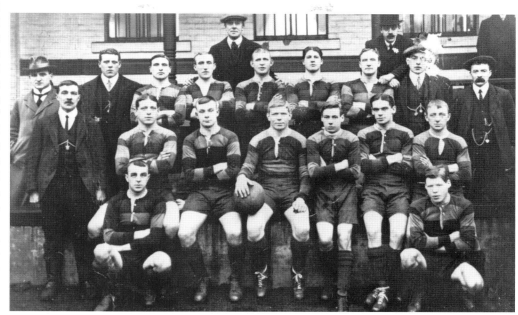

Below: On 7 May, 1949, Bradford Northern created a record by visiting Wembley in the final for the third consecutive year. The team consisted of practically the same players each year and was captained on each occasion by Ernest Ward, The team was: Leake, Batten, Kitchen, E Ward, Edwards, Davies, D Ward, Whitcombe,

Northern won 12-0, with tries from Batten and Davies. Captain fantastic, Ernest Ward, received the Lance Todd Trophy, as man of the match. On Monday 9 May, a tumultuous reception greeted the team on their triumphant return for a well-deserved civic reception at the Town Hall.

Fabulous speedway action from 1947, approximately two years after the Bradford club was originally formed. At the time the club was known as the Bradford Boomerangs. Seen here on the right is Alec Statham, as he bid to hold off the challenge from West Ham's Malcolm Craven, alongside. The post war period was a boom time for speedway, with crowds of over 20,000 attending regularly at Odsal. The high point was the 47,050 who saw England defeat Australia 65-43 on 5 July 1947, a figure that remains the highest crowd for a speedway meeting at Odsal. In the 50s, the team name changed to Bradford Tudors and changed again in the early 60s to Panthers. The club unfortunately folded in 1962. It reformed in 1970 as Bradford Northern, until the club folded once again in 1976, after a two year spell as the 'Barons'. The greatest spell of success came in the 80s and 90s, when the Halifax Dukes were offered a new home at Odsal. During this period, the team won eight Championships and a world title, until the club's closure in 1997 for the third and final time, despite winning the Elite League Championship.

In speedway's 84-year history, only six English riders have become World Speedway Champion and Gary Havelock achieved this as a Bradford rider in 1992. Havelock spent ten seasons at the Bradford Dukes after a move from his local club, Middlesbrough Tigers, in 1987.

Speedway popularity, thanks to Sky television, has increased at an incredible rate and it is now apparently the third most televised sport in the UK.

Did you know?

Bradford was the location for the films Yanks, starring Richard Gere, and The Railway Children, a 1970s classic starring Jenny Agutter, and featured in Monty Python's ground-breaking 1983 film 'The Meaning of Life', with footage filmed in Lister Park.

in physical education. She also held on to the view that a good win was better than a good defeat. Sister Gabriel put away her boots in the summer and picked up her umpire's coat as she also coached the cricket team.

Below: The picturesque Lister Park (also known as Manningham Park) started life started life as the estate of Samual Cunliffe Lister. Bradford Corporation bought the estate in 1870 and it has become Bradford's most popular park. Lister's mansion house was demolished and Cartwright Hall was built on the site. The park has been successfully renovated in recent years. The lake has been re-opened for boats and a Mughal Water Garden constructed. There are also tennis and basketball courts, bowling greens and a children's playground. In 2006, it was given the prestigious award of Britain's Best Park, and was also nominated for Best Park in Europe. In this picture we can see crowds of people enjoying a sunny day near the main entrance. On the way into the park they pass the statue of Samuel Lister, Lord Masham. The statue (by Matthew Noble) was raised in 1875.

Above: On me 'ead, son, or in this case sister. It is September 1965 and the St Joseph's team is being put through its paces by Sister Gabriel in a spot of pre-season training. The art of trapping the ball was being demonstrated to some of the lads who were pupils at the school on Park Lane, near St Luke's Hospital. The nun took sport very seriously, regarding it as an important part of character building as well as its obvious influence

This is a fabulous view from Northcliffe Gardens in Shipley, looking across the valley towards Wrose. In the distance we are looking at Prospect Mount as it climbs up towards Carr Lane, and on the right, Gaisby Lane and Bolton Woods Quarry. Nearer to the camera we look down on the A650 Bradford Road as it crosses from left to right towards Frizinghall. The view has changed very little today, with the parade of shops that still include the Cosy Clifton Café, on the corner of Norwood Place. The allotments on the right may have disappeared but the beautifully well manicured park has long been a haven of peace for the people of Shipley. It could well be school holiday time as these three young lads sit in the spring sunshine on the sloping grassland near to Cliffe Wood Avenue. Today, this parkland area is even more picturesque than it was then, as it has been naturally landscaped with colourful trees, bushes and rocks.

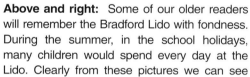

Above and right: Some of our older readers will remember the Bradford Lido with fondness. During the summer, in the school holidays, many children would spend every day at the Lido. Clearly from these pictures we can see that it is sunny and warm as all the children are out in their swimming cossies. There are few days in the average Yorkshire year that are warm enough to brave the elements, but fortunately for all this is one of them, although

the water was probably freezing. The Lido was Bradford's only outdoor swimming pool and was built in Lister Park in 1930. Tom Daley would have had a great time as there was a variety of diving boards at different heights. For the less brave, you could go down the slide into the water or just jump in from the side. Sadly, not every day was a summer's day and when spending cutbacks in the 1970s were on the agenda, it was not surprising that the Lido was near the top of the list. The open air pool closed in 1973. An attempt to reopen the Lido in the 80s, was scuppered by the council because of the amount of repairs and restoration work needed to bring it up to standard. A sad loss to the city, it was demolished in 1991.

Left: This is a pretty scenic view of Peel Park from the 1950s. Peel Park has a mixture of attractions and was Bradford's first public park, named after Sir Robert Peel. After money was raised from public and private donations, it was opened to the public for the first time in 1853. A series of galas were held in the park to raise funds to pay off the remaining debt for the purchase of the land, which took some 12 years in total. In 1870, the park was conveyed to the Municipal Borough of Bradford and is now owned by the City of Bradford. In the 1900s, the park lake had a large ornamental fountain and a footbridge crossing the water, which we can see clearly in this photograph. In 1902, an ornamental bandstand was erected midway along the terrace, but today this location is occupied by the statue of Sir Robert Peel. Another lost feature is the two cannons captured by the British in the Crimean War. Today the park is the scene of the Bradford Mela which is a large-scale celebration principally of South Asian culture, and was the first such event in Europe. It takes place in the events area in the far north east of the park. In 1997, Bradford City's centenary year, 100 trees were planted in the park and this is commemorated by a stone plaque on a boulder near the southern entrance.

Above: Yes, this is a rare photograph of the late, great, actress and singer Dame Gracie Fields, on a visit to Bradford in the mid-1930s. She is seen here looking resplendent, leaning against this classic sports car outside Cartwright Hall. Born over a fish and chip shop in Rochdale, her down to earth manner and humble beginnings made her a firm favourite with audiences. Her most famous song, which became her theme, "Sally," was worked into the title of her first film, Sally in Our Alley (1931), which was a major box office hit. It is believed she may have been in Bradford filming a scene in 'Look Up And Laugh', which is thought to use Kirkgate Market as a backdrop. The plot features Gracie leading market stallholders against a chain store which is trying to have the market closed down. The discovery of an ancient Royal Charter saves the day. On its release, the film was first shown in Bradford at both the Regent and the Savoy from Monday, 11 November, 1935.

Did you know?

Jim Laker (1922–1986) was a Surrey and England cricketer, born in Frizinghall.

Bottom left: He may have captained England, but Len Hutton did not have airs and graces. He still found time to lend a hand in his Town Hall Square sports shop. In 1953, he was approaching the end of his career as a professional cricketer; hence the need to make sure that he had something else that could provide an income when he hung up his pads for the last time. Born in 1916, he made his Yorkshire debut in 1934. By 1937, he was in the Test team and astounded statisticians when scoring 364 in a single innings against Australia. This was a world record that stood for nearly 20 years. Hutton became the England captain in 1952 and, in the year that this photograph was taken, led his side to win the Ashes. He was knighted in 1956 and became Yorkshire president shortly before his death in 1990.

Below: The days have long gone since we saw performing seals, dog acts, snarling lions, elephants doing dainty pirouettes and prancing horses. Now, circuses are little more than showcases for acrobats, wire walkers and girls swinging around on ribbons. In the mid-1960s we could still see a proper show under the Big Top. When Billy Smart came to town we would have a parade of stilt walkers, clowns, jugglers and a whole host of animals drawn from all over the globe. Billy Smart was a showman and fairground proprietor who bought a circus in 1946. With the help of his ten children, the show became one of the best of its type in the land.

In the late 1930s Broadway was developed into a major new shopping street occupying a prime position at the junction of Broadway and Leeds Road. This gave the John Maxwell (ABC) group the best chance of competing with rival New Victoria cinema/theatre complex and the new Odeon. The Ritz opened on the evening of 8 May 1939, with a large invited guest list that included the Mayor and Mayoress of Bradford. This photograph of the queues outside the ABC cinema is from November 1974. The cinema had been converted into a triple screen, after the single screen cinema had closed a few months earlier. This was probably the opening of screens 2 & 3 on 18 November, 1974. Two weeks later the Minors' Matinee on Saturday mornings was reintroduced and they continued every Saturday morning with admission only 10 pence. Cannon took over the EMI-ABC in 1986 but their ownership was short-lived, as the cinema closed on 17 September 1987. Perhaps appropriately the final film in ABC1 was 'Rita, Sue and Bob Too', based on the play by Bradford playwright Andrea Dunbar and filmed around Bradford and Baildon.

Did you know?

Bradford was the home of Pablo Fanque, the popular black Victorian circus owner and performer, whose poster advertisement inspired John Lennon to write The Beatles' Being for the Benefit of Mr. Kite!.

BUILDINGS & MONUMENTS

Right: This statue of Sir Titus Salt, founder of the model village of Saltaire and its textile mills, sits proudly at the Norman Arch entrance to Lister Park. The elaborate canopy was designed by Lockwood and Mawson and was carved by the Westminster firm of Farmer and Brindley. The statue itself was carved from a block of white Carrara marble which originally weighed about 14 tons. It was unveiled on 1 August 1874 by the seventh Duke of Devonshire. The statue was apparently moved from the original site in front of the Town Hall, to its current location, because of the increase in traffic, and was unveiled for a second time on 17 August 1896. Titus Salt at one point had five mills and was the biggest employer in Bradford. Uniquely among millowners, he was a philanthropist and a socialist. He established the model town of Saltaire in which all the workers had good houses and built the model 'Salts Mill' with the best workplace conditions in Yorkshire. In December 2001, Saltaire was designated a World Heritage Site by UNESCO.

Bottom left and below: The building with the rounded cupola is Britannia House, seemingly festooned with cabling for the tram and trolley ways. In the accompanying picture, the Town Hall can be seen in all its majesty. Britannia House, on the corner of Bridge Street and Hall Ings, is an imposing multi-storey municipal building of 1,170 square yards of ground floor space. It also has a number of retail outlets below its floors of offices. The Town Hall was designed by Lockwood and Mawson and opened in 1873 as a result of a competition to create a municipal building that would rival the mighty buildings that adorned the centres of Leeds and Halifax. It was extended in 1909 when another council chamber, committee rooms and a banqueting hall were added. A new entrance and staircase were created in 1914.

It was renamed City Hall in 1965. The impressive bell tower, from which a peal is heard on the quarter hour, stands 220 feet high. However, the clock was not added until 1937. Students of royal history might be able to recognise the 35 past monarchs whose statues adorn the exterior. Bizarrely, they include a figure of the arch republican, Oliver Cromwell.

Did you know?

There are well over 5,500 listed buildings in Bradford.

Right: This is one of the oldest buildings in the city and parts of it date from the 14th century. Now a museum and education centre, Bolling Hall was possibly once some form of fortified keep as it occupies an elevated position on the outskirts of Bradford and, in earlier times, would have had defensive potential. During the 17th century Civil War, the hall was used as a Royalist base. Supposedly, a ghost appeared during this occupation and spoke to the Earl of Newcastle, saying, 'Pity poor Bradford'. The hall is named after William Bolling, who acquired the manor in 1316. Today, Bolling Hall's exhibits include period bedroom furniture, along with a Civil War room that contains Oliver Cromwell's death mask.

Below: A view of Bradford Childrens Hospital, built in 1883 as a dedicated hospital for children. The building in St Mary's Road is an imposing stone structure with two-storey 'turreted' annex. It closed after 105 years, in 1988, subsequently being used for a number of years as a nursing and residential home. The attractive and imposing Grade II listed building is now part of the Manningham Conservation Area.

Right: Now an art gallery and museum, the Cartwright Hall was built in 1900-03 to J W Simpson and M Allen's competition-winning design. It is a grand neo-Baroque building of very fine quality ashlar masonary. The hall was opened and dedicated by Lord Masham in 1904, with a collection of Victorian and Edwardian works donated by Samuel Lister. Cartwright Hall is the centrepiece of Lister Park and played the same role at the 1904 Bradford Industrial Exhibition, which was held in the park. The hall is named after Dr Edmund Cartwright and was seen as a most fitting tribute to Cartwright, who, by inventing the power loom and the combing machine, had played such a large part in Bradford's rise to fame and prosperity. The building was given Grade II listed status by English Heritage in June 1963 and enjoys scenic views across the city.

Below: A quiet day on Horton Road in 1943 gives a clear view of the Technical School and Art School. The former was opened by the Prince and Princess of Wales on 23 June, 1882. The future King Edward VII and Queen Alexandra had travelled from Saltaire Station past enthusiastic crowds lining the streets for the whole of the four-mile journey. The royal couple were impressed by an exhibition of the finest art, textiles and machine innovations mounted in their honour. To the right is the 1877 former Mannville New Connection Chapel. This is now Grove Library.

Did you know?

Ron Wing CBE was a leading pharmacist who launched Ibuprofen and was instrumental in providing new treatments for epilepsy. He studied as an apprentice at Bradford Technical College from 1942 to 1947.

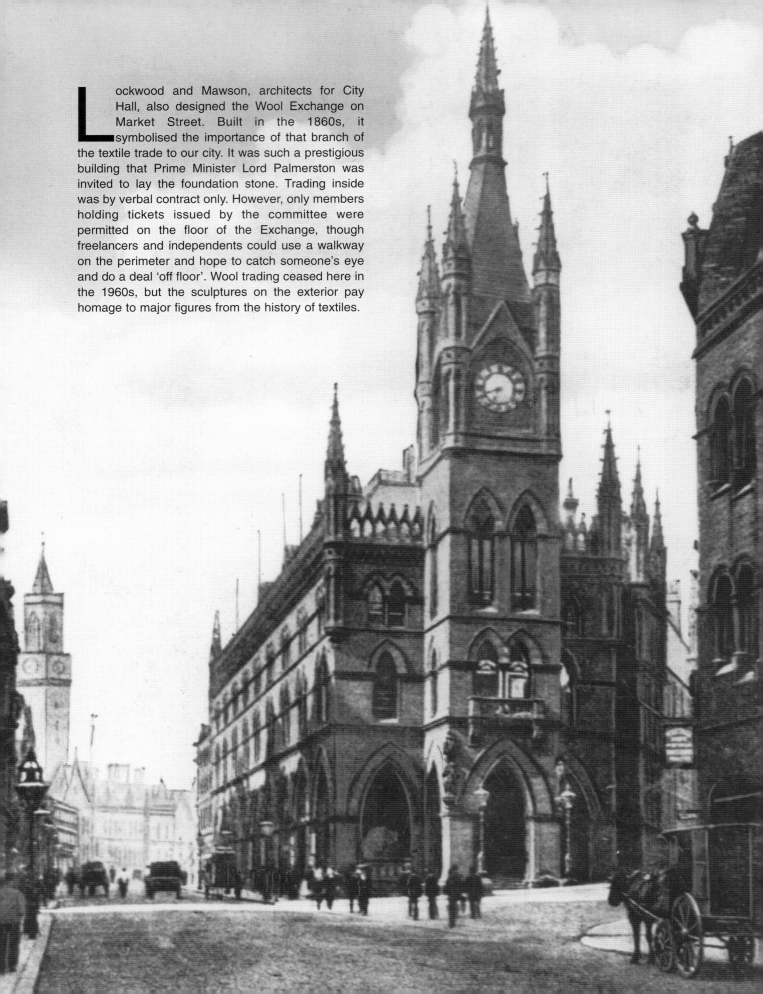

Lockwood and Mawson, architects for City Hall, also designed the Wool Exchange on Market Street. Built in the 1860s, it symbolised the importance of that branch of the textile trade to our city. It was such a prestigious building that Prime Minister Lord Palmerston was invited to lay the foundation stone. Trading inside was by verbal contract only. However, only members holding tickets issued by the committee were permitted on the floor of the Exchange, though freelancers and independents could use a walkway on the perimeter and hope to catch someone's eye and do a deal 'off floor'. Wool trading ceased here in the 1960s, but the sculptures on the exterior pay homage to major figures from the history of textiles.

produced. A steam locomotive was even named Silver Jubilee in honour of the occasion.

Bottom: This was the changing face of city centre shopping around Broadway in the late 1960s and 1970s. What was once a city with an almost exclusively Victorian set of buildings altered as the result of a seduction by modernist thinking of the day. Known to some as brutalism, architecture of that era depended upon rectangular geometry created by lengths of concrete, steel and glass. There was not a castellation, turret, gargoyle or little bit of individuality in sight. This was not just a Bradfordian scene as you could have lifted up every C and A, WH Smith or H Samuel and dropped them into any other city centre without noticing. The shopping and visual experience became identical whatever town you visited.

Above: The gas showrooms on Leeds Road, or what is now Broadway, were decorated patriotically with union flags and images of King George V and Queen Mary. Since it was 1935, it is fairly safe to assume that the display was mounted to mark the occasion of the Silver Jubilee. They had become popular members of the royal family, despite their Germanic roots. The couple had made their Britishness a formal matter when they abandoned the family name of Saxe-Coburg Gotha in 1917, replacing it with Windsor. To mark 25 years on the throne, medals, stamps, coins, cups and other memorabilia were

Did you know?

The Hepolite Company, situated in Bradford at St John's works manufacturing plant, designed and developed internal combustion engines and components.

Left: That the Alhambra remains one of Bradford's most distinctive buildings is testimony to the bold and extraordinary design undertaken. Built at a cost of £20,000 for theatre impresario Francis Laidler, who already owned two music halls, the new Alhambra Theatre was opened on Wednesday 18 March, 1914. Laidler, who later became known as the 'King of Pantomime', accumulated his wealth in Bradford's brewing and wool industries, but his real passion was the theatre. In 1964 Bradford City Council bought the Alhambra and ten years later it was designated a Grade II listed building. Built originally by Chadwick and Watson, it was restored to its former grandeur in 1986, after a period of

uncertainty when it looked as if it might be demolished. Today, with an overall seating capacity in excess of 1,400, the Alhambra is a major touring venue and hosts a wide range of stage shows from ballet and opera to variety and comedy, musicals, drama and, of course, the annual pantomime. The Alhambra theatre has been the home of pantomime for many years (he's behind you…oh no he's not), and still is.

Left and above: The Midland Hotel, Lower Kirkgate, on the opposite side of Cheapside, marks the approach to the former Midland Station (Forster Square), which was built between 1885 and 1890 by the Midland Railway Company. The architect was Charles Trubshaw, who was contracted to design many stations for the Company. The Hotel was a showpiece for the railway company's northern operations, and is of particular architectural interest, with one of the finest Victorian interiors in the city. The architecture of the building is both breathtaking and inspiring, blending to make you appreciate the opulence of an era unfortunately long past. The Midland Hotel is owned and managed by London based Peel Hotels. There is a significant amount of history attached to the hotel, due principally to the fact that it played host to the rich and famous during its heyday, including Laurel and Hardy, Paul Robeson, The Beatles and the Rolling Stones. In 1905, the famous Shakespearean stage actor, Sir Henry Irving died on the main staircase after his appearance at the nearby Theatre Royal. He was attended by his manager Bram Stoker, better known as the originator of Dracula. Almost every Prime Minister up to Harold Wilson stayed in the hotel. Looking at the cars in this photograph we would estimate the date to be around the mid-1980s, with parking available in what was once the city's main railway station. At the time, the station had six platforms covered by an overall glazed roof and a Victorian walkway linking the hotel to the platforms. Following the "golden age of steam" the hotel fell into disrepair until it was bought by Bradford entrepreneur John Pennington in 1992, who restored it and the hotel re-opened as the Pennington Midland Hotel the following year. It was sold to Peel Hotels in December 1998, who then returned to its original name.

Below and right: Town Hall square in the 1940s, compared with the 1960s, looked much the same. Tarmac had replaced setts in many places and traffic was on the increase, but the main fabric of the city centre was much as it was. Although it has now become Centenary Square and the ground level furniture is much more modern and the vista includes screens and water features, this is still Bradford's heartland. City Hall provides a backdrop of grandeur and gravitas to all that happens infront of it. It was 1847 when Queen Victoria signed a charter that brought Bradford, Manningham, Bowling and Horton together as a single borough. The first council members met in the Fire Station House on Swain Street for 26 years until the purpose-built Town Hall was erected by the Shipley company, John Ives and Son, at a cost of £100,000. The ceremonial opening took place on 9 September, 1873, performed by the Mayor, Alderman Matthew Thompson. In 1997, Bradford celebrated its centenary as a city and the name of this area, that had been Town Hall Square and subsequently City Square, became Centenary Square. It is now one of the pedestrianised parts of Bradford.

Did you know?

Bradford Grammar School was in existence near the parish church in the mid-16th century and re-established by Royal Charter as the Free Grammar School of Charles II in 1662.

largest in the Oscar Deutsch chain with 2,713 seats, when it originally opened on 17 December 1938. It was a sad day for cinemagoers when it closed, as the city had lost another of its three grand 'super-cinemas'. The chapel itself was soon to be a casualty of the bulldozer in order to make way for the new Magistrates' Court. The Odeon site was to become the Police Headquarters in an area to be known as The Tyrls. An underground passageway was apparently built between the two buildings for the transferring of prisoners from cell to courtroom.

Below: Fronting Town Hall Square, is the solitary building of the Unitarian Chapel, built in 1869. We can date this image to 1969, as in the background, behind the chapel, we can see the demolition of the Odeon on Manchester Road. The Oddfellows Arms, next door to the cinema, had been demolished earlier to make way for the new Jacob's Well roundabout and subway passages. In its day, the Bradford Odeon was the

Did you know?

John William Gott (1866–1922) from Bradford, was the last person in Britain to be tried for blasphemy.

EVENTS & OCCASIONS

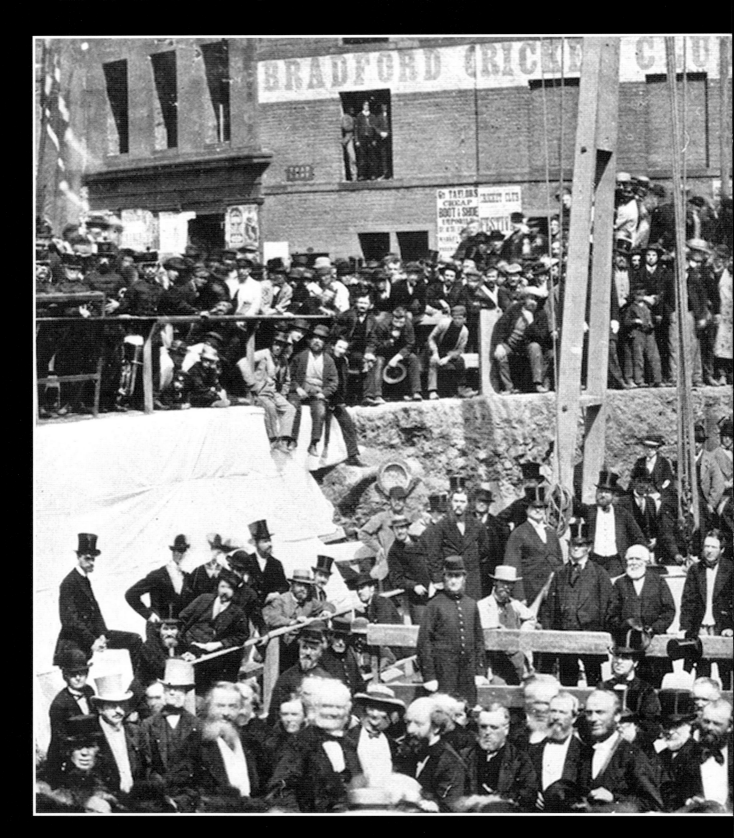

Left: The first town hall in Bradford was sited in the Fire Station House in Swain Street, in 1847. This remained the Town Hall for twenty-six years. As the town grew in population and prosperity it became clear that a purpose built civic building was needed and in 1869 the present triangular site was purchased. A competition to design the town hall was held and thirty-two entries were received. The winning design was submitted by Lockwood and Mawson, a Bradford firm of architects. The builder was John Ives & Son of Shipley and took three years to complete. In this photograph we can see the large crowds at the laying of the foundation stone ceremony in August 1870. All the various public bodies were represented, including the Mayor, Mark Dawson and a large majority of the leading men in Bradford at the time also attended the ceremony. A large group of invited dignitaries assembled at the Corporation offices in Swaine Street and at noon, they marched in procession to the new site. The building was completed three years later and opened by the Mayor, Alderman Matthew Thompson on 9 September 1873.

Above: Bradford's most famous landmark - the 220ft high clock tower has dominated the skyline since the days before high-rise buildings. The tower is Italianate, inspired by the Palazzo Vecchio in Florence. It has thirteen bells which were installed at a cost of £5,000. The total weight of the bells is 17 tons and the largest of the bells can be seen here during the mammoth installation project in 1873. A large group of men have stopped to pose for this rare photograph, as the massive bell is readied for its entrance into the building. Rather unusually this bell was given the name 'Big Matthew William', after the Mayor, Alderman Thompson, who performed the opening ceremony in 1873. Workers were given a holiday

Wow!!! have you ever seen a more interesting and frankly, dangerous looking photograph. Every vantage point has been taking, people are hanging out of windows and some are even sitting on the very edge of the surrounding rooftops.The crowds are swarming on mass on the ground as they make their way through Victoria Square towards the Town Hall. It is believed this photograph is linked to the Royal visit the Prince and Princess of Wales. The future King and Queen were here to officially open the Bradford Exhibition on 4 May, 1904. On a fine day they travelled by train from Arthington to Bradford, where they were greeted by huge crowds who lined the route to Lister Park. After touring the Exhibition the Royal Party left for Victoria Square, where the Prince unveiled Alfred Drury's statue of the late Queen.

Below: So working on the railways is a man's job? Don't you believe it. During World War I, when the lads went off to fight overseas, their places on the shop floor, in munitions industries, behind the steering wheels, in the fields and carrying out heavy manual work were taken over by the so-called weaker sex. The female workforce grouped on the 4-4-2 High Flyer locomotive, No 1406, were employed by the Lancashire and Yorkshire Railway Company. They were based at the Low Moor engine shed and more than did their bit for King and country.

Right: It is hard to get a feel from this snapshot of the Bradford Historical Pageant of the scale of the event and the efforts of Bradfordians for the pageant to even take place. The overall contribution is mind boggling with an estimated tenth of the population having a direct hand in the event over the six months of its planning and execution, including the making of 7,500 costumes. Events included historical re-enactments in Peel Park as well as processions through the city and evening bonfire celebrations. The event took place from 13-18 July, 1931, with the hope that the publicity generated by this and the prestigious Imperial Wool Industries Fair, would boost business in Bradford, after the financial crash of 1929 and the worldwide depression that followed. Such was the interest, that HRH Prince George performed the opening ceremony. What we can see in this photograph is groups of people dancing around in circles holding hands, as a preamble to a re-enactment of a battle from the English Civil War.

Bottom right: Those of us who recall Elizabeth Bowes-Lyon (1900-2002) as the old 'Queen Mum' forget that she was one of the society belles of the post-First World War years. She had many suitors and, somewhat reluctantly, agreed to marry the then Duke of York, the future George VI, in 1923. Her reservations were simply based on being so much in the public eye, but, people took to her quite readily as everyone was wooed by her charm and grace. This was evident during a visit the couple made to

G Garnett and Sons, the woollen and worsted manufacturer based at Apperley Bridge. The Duchess was a strong willed woman who soon learned to take charge on such occasions as her husband, to her right, was nervous of taking centre stage.

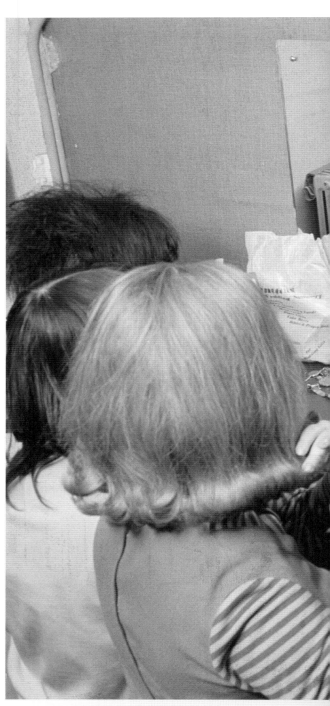

Above: Viewed here in all its classical splendour is the New Victoria. Erected on the site of the old William Whittaker's brewery, the citadel fronted building had not been open for very long when this photograph was taken in 1931. In the 1930s Bradford was a growing, busy and very prosperous city and the luxurious 3,500 seater New Victoria complete with ballroom, restaurant and tearoom/cafe was a spectacular showpiece. Such was the interest in the William Illingworth designed building, that the Prince of Wales requested a private viewing on one of his visits to Bradford. The ballroom was situated above the restaurant on the Thornton Road side of the building. Music was provided by The New Victoria Melody 5 and later by the hugely popular Billy Hey and His Band, who enjoyed a 22-years residency here. In September 1950, the name was changed to the Gaumont. Sadly, after a period of audience decline, the Gaumont closed its doors on 30 November, 1968.

Below: Give yourself a pat on the back if you can identify these four young girls looking in the mirror, backstage at the Bradford Gaumont in October, 1964. From left to right they are: Jamaican-born Millie Small, better known as 'Millie' of 'My Boy Lollipop' fame, Megan Davies, female bass player of The Applejacks, Lulu, real name Marie Lawrie, and Honey Lantree of The Honeycombs, one of the few female drummers in Britain at that time. Unbelievably, Lulu was only fifteen in this photograph, having been thrust into the limelight following the success of her debut single 'Shout'.

The girls were getting ready for rehearsals at the Gaumont, having been thrown together as part of the "The Big Beat Scene", which was a non-stop pop spectacular touring the country. The Gaumont Cinema was a also a significant venue for The Beatles. In addition to being one of only two venues in the north of England to stage a preview concert of The Beatles Christmas Show, they also opened their first UK tour there in February 1963. It was the choice for the start of their 1964 British Tour when 6,000 screaming fans greeted the group as Beatlemania swept across the country.

ON THE MOVE

system was still less expensive to run than the tramways and it was more suited to less densely populated routes. Not very originally, "Trackless" was the Bradford name for these vehicles, which started running from Latimer Street. Interestingly, the driver had a windscreen but no door – and the final drive was provided by chains. Trolley buses ceased to be run in 1972, in the city that pioneered them.

Top right: The tram route to Heaton from Forster Square, via North Park Road, ended outside the Kings Arms in Highgate. Seen here in old photograph from 1907, the tramcar has a 'Bellamy Top' which covered about two thirds of

Above: A fine example of innovation in public transport, is this Hurst Nelson solid tyred trolley bus at Laisterdyke around 1912. The Tramways Department decided to investigate the possibilities of a trackless tram system in 1909 when they visited various up-and-running systems on the Continent. Bradford and Leeds were the first cities in the United Kingdom to adopt them. The vehicles for the route cost £5,500 and the other necessary electrical equipment etc. totalled £9,000. Even so, the trolley bus

the upper deck. Over a hundred years later the Kings Arms is still going strong, next door to the Post Office in Heaton. The tram is carrying an advertisement for Holloway's pills and ointments. Holloway's business was extremely successful. A key factor in his enormous success in business was advertising, in which he had great faith. By the time of his death, in 1883, he was spending over £50,000 a year on advertising his products. The sales of his products made him

a multi-millionaire, and one of the richest men in Britain at the time. Holloway's products were said to be able to cure a whole host of ailments, though scientific evaluation of them after his death showed that few of them contained any ingredients which would be considered to be of significant medicinal value. The tram route to Horton finished in 1935.

Below: We jet in and out of Leeds-Bradford Airport quite merrily nowadays as we whiz off to all points of the compass. Yet, there was a time when air travel was just a pipe dream for the man in the street. These aeroplanes would have been privately owned and a mixture of small commercial enterprises and playthings for the monied classes. Yeadon Aerodrome, as it was then known, began operating in 1931 as a base for club flying and training. Scheduled flights began in 1935 and included

destinations like Manchester and Newcastle. The nearest we got to foreign holidays was a service to such exotic destinations as Edinburgh or the Isle of Man! Civil flights were suspended during the war, only being reinstated in 1947. Leeds-Bradford was upgraded to a regional airport in 1978 and was greatly redeveloped in the next decade.

Did you know

Since flying began on the Leeds-Bradford International airfield in 1931, the Airport has grown to offer flights to over 65 destinations serving approximately 2.6 million passengers a year.

Above and top right: Tower wagons were used by tramways companies to assist with the maintenance of overhead wires. In later years, they would also be of assistance when attending to repairs on street lighting. The Milnes-Daimler vehicle (above), dating from the early 1900s, was undergoing a test programme before entering full-time service. The later model, a Karrier built for the Corporation in the summer of 1947, was still doing good work 15 years later. However, it was withdrawn from operational work at the end of 1962. Karriers were manufactured by Clayton and Company, a Huddersfield firm that, after early production of motorcars, concentrated on public transport and commercial vehicles.

Right: Ever since organised transport services started in Bradford in 1882, the streets have witnessed the passage of horse trams, steam trams, electric trams, trolley buses and motor buses. In this picture we can see a trolley bus and a tram together at Bankfoot. Bradford trolleybus 507 is about to leave Bankfoot terminus for Laisterdyke, on what was an extension of the UK and Bradford's first trolley bus route from Dudley Hill to Laisterdyke. It is hard to tell from the image, but this could be Mayo Avenue, with Tram 81 waiting to pick up passengers in Manchester Road, going across from left to right.

Above: How far can you lean a 1930s Bradford double-decker trolley bus before it falls over? The answer lies here in the test centre, and appears to be about 37 degrees. Before going into service, all buses undergo extensive safety tests. One of these is the tilt test, which tests the stability of the bus in poor conditions. The top deck is loaded with sandbags to represent the weight of the passengers. The vehicle is then gradually tilted to a minimum angle of 28 degrees. All the wheels of the bus must stay in contact with the road in order to pass the test. This trolley bus was made by English Electric and is fleet number 575 and entered service in 1929, with registration number KW 6065. It was withdrawn around 1945.

Right: It is very rare to see a photograph of bus with an external staircase. This West Yorkshire Transport Leyland bus probably dates from around 1930. The bus was part of a fleet of buses operated by the West Yorkshire Road Car Company. This company was formed in 1928, after the Harrogate Road Car Company merged with Blythe and Berwick, of Bradford. Eagle-eyed Bradfordians will recognise that the classic double-decker is rounding the island in Forster Square. Further evidence are the two Ford Royal Mail vans parked outside the post office. The 1930 Model A pickup sold for the equivalent of $395. If any more proof was needed we can see the clock tower of the cathedral in the back of shot, with the time at 4.15pm. The signpost to the left for the 'Aerodrome', relates to Leeds Bradford International Airport (LBA), which was originally Yeadon Aerodrome and began operating in October 1931 with club flying and training flights being predominant activities.

Right: A splendid example for all trolley bus enthusiasts, of an English Electric type E11 at Saltaire. The bus is about to start on the return route to Bradford via Thackley. This particular model came into service in Bradford in 1931 and was withdrawn in 1942. Bradford had a superb and very interesting trolley bus system and was well-suited to trolley bus operation as the topography of the area is rather like a bowl, meaning that almost every route involved a sustained climb out of the city. Leeds and Bradford became the first cities to put trolley buses into service in Great Britain on 20 June, 1911. Bradford was also the last to operate trolley buses in the UK, the system closing on 26 March, 1972. The last rear-entrance trolley bus in Britain was also in Bradford and is now owned by the Bradford Trolley bus Association.

Did you know?

Jowett Cars, founded by the Jowett brothers in 1909 in Bradford, was one of the early companies of the British motor industry. The Jowett brothers invented a new engine to be used in automobiles and their goal was to provide a low weight vehicle at an affordable price and with low running costs.

Above: A picture from 1949, near the end of tram operations, on the Horton Top – Queensbury route. On the right we can see the WYRCC Bristol 308 leaving Chester Street Bus Station on its way to Otley.

Left and above: The tramcar heading for Odsal, home of Bradford Northern rugby league team, operated along the No 15 route. Behind it, the Kellett Woodman textiles building can be seen. Photographed on 22 April, 1950, the tram service had only a few years of life left in it. The companion image was taken on a Town Hall Square that still boasted some delightful granite setts. Both trams carried adverts for beverages on their fronts. Everyone knows about Bovril, but younger readers may not recall the Ramsden name. This was a company of brewers based until the early 1960s in the centre of Halifax at Ward's End, where it had been established in the mid-19th century as the Stone Trough Brewery.

something extra special about the company that was one of the founders of the British motor industry. In 1906, Bradford brothers Benjamin and William Jowett designed and built their first car, however, full production did not start until 1910. A new site, on a disused quarry at Springfield Road, Idle, was purchased as the base for their new works premises, almost ten years later. Undoubtedly, there are still many families in Bradford whose fathers, brothers, uncles and grandfathers worked for the company. With names like Jupiter, Javelin and Flying Fox, they are certainly cars which, when people see them, evoke memories of their childhood.

Above and below: Jowett is still a name to conjure with among fans of vintage vehicles years after the last one rolled off the production line in 1954. To the people of Bradford there is Jowett still has a loyal and proud following, and the Jowett Car Club is probably the oldest one-make car club in the world, having been founded in 1923.

Bottom: Seen in 1969, the driver and conductor of this Bradford Corporation bus were indulging in a few moments' rest before setting off for Shelf, the village on the way to Halifax that was the birthplace of soccer star Frank Worthington and TV presenters Linda Barker and John Noakes. The bus is a Leyland Titan, a very popular make. Different generations of this vehicle were in production from the 1920s right up to the end of the 1960s. Titans were so successful that they were seen as far afield as India as the Ashok Leyland Titans and, it is said, at least one bus saw service in Indonesia.

Above: Newbould's had bakeries at Dick Lane, Bradford and in Sheffield. Here, one of its vans was parked up at the Exchange. The station which opened in May, 1850, on the south side of Hall Ings as a joint venture by the Lancashire and Yorkshire and Great Northern Railway Companies. The popularity of this form of travel meant that the Exchange could not cope with the volume of passengers wishing to use the service, so the old station was demolished and replaced on the same site by a new one in 1880. There were ten bays, under two arched, wrought iron roofs. Business fell dramatically in the 1960s and the Exchange was replaced by a new four platform station, built about 50 yards away, in 1973.

> ## Did you know?
>
> *Edward Spurr (1907–1998) was an inventor who was brought up in Eccleshill. He designed a powerboat engine with Lawrence of Arabia, worked on the Dambusters' bouncing bomb and Frank Whittle's jet engine.*

Below and right: This pair of AEC Regent III buses were heading out of the city in the middle of the last century. The Hebble service to Halifax left Chester Street bus station along the No 17 route. This particular model was introduced in 1949, but withdrawn three years later. The corresponding picture of the No 74 leaving Town Hall Square, with the Burton building on the corner of Tyrell Street to its left, shows the bus off to Horton Bank Top. Bradford Corporation only introduced its own motorbus service after the First World War. There had been a long running legal dispute with the West Riding Automobile Company before the Corporation could gain a licence to run its own fleet. In the mid-1920s there were at least a dozen, if not more, private bus operators all attempting to get some sort of upper hand over their competitors. Bradford, though, could use its financial muscle to add buses of greater capacity to its fleet and gradually gain control of the market. What had been largely a single decker service was expanded as along came the double deckers. These, together with the trolley buses, also accelerated the demise of the tramways.

Below: Bradford's love affair with trolley buses lasted longer than any other town or city in Britain. Yet, all good things come to an end. On Sunday, 28 March, 1972, the last journey by these vehicles was made into the Thornbury depot. To mark the occasion, a number of specials provided the public with nostalgic tours along the route. Here, a trio of such vehicles had arrived on Leeds Road and were only yards away from ending their careers. It was way back on 20 June, 1911, that the first service from Laisterdyke to Dudley Hill had begun when two single decker Railless chassis vehicles with Hurst Nelson B28R bodies collected their first passengers.

AT WORK

Right: A very clean, calm and serene view of backroom workers beavering away behind the scenes at Busby's famous department store. In the days before household washing machines, the chore of doing the family washing on a regular basis was not the most popular task undertaken by the majority of housewives, hence the term 'washday blues'. This could explain this scene in Busby's laundry department where washing, ironing and clothes alteration service was available. Rows of industrial washing machines can be seen down the left-hand side of the room, with a single driveshaft overhead powering the machines by belt drive. The overseer is sitting at her desk in the foreground looking on. Her reputation would be that of quite a stern woman, so not much chance of any slacking or frivolity whilst she was in the room.

Bottom left: This photograph from the late 1940s shows a weaving shed in Bradford, crammed full of 'Northop' worsted looms. Before the electric motor was developed to the state where each loom had its own independent power source, a series of shafts would be built into the ceiling of the weaving shed, with rubber belts taking the power to each loom. The ladies seen working at the looms would need to be highly skilled, with a strong sense of manual dexterity in order to keep up with the running speed of the machines.

Below: Workers' playtime, and after a hard day's work at Salts Mills - the largest employer in Shipley - it's clocking off time, and workers eager for a good meal and 'Double Your Money' head for the great outdoors. Known in the old days as 't'penny oile', this particular gateway was where workers of old paid a penny fine if they were late for work - and in the days of early starts and no alarm clocks, getting to work on time was a fine art. No 'penny oile' of course in the 1950s when this scene was captured - just black looks for any latecomer from the overlooker!

Joseph A. Hey & Son Ltd
Fitting Farewells

There are only two certainties: death and taxes. Taxes can sometimes be avoided, but no one avoids life's last act. The passing of a loved one can present many problems, but with the professional help of an experienced Funeral Director those difficulties can be met and resolved with complete confidence.

Funeral Directors Joseph A. Hey & Son Ltd, based in Great Horton Road, was established in Bradford in 1908, though its family roots go back even earlier, to the 1860s. Today the company is still an independent family owned and managed business. Joan (Jo) Hey Morphet holds a Diploma in Funeral Directing. She is part of the fourth generation of the family working in the firm and is the Company Secretary and Director. The company's business interests now extend to Monumental Masonry, with two separate companies importing directly from the country of origin and the development supply of innovative award winning environmentally friendly coffins and caskets. In 1990, Robert Morphet was appointed Managing Director having worked in the funeral profession since leaving school in 1980. He holds a Diploma in Funeral Directing, a Diploma in

Management Studies and is a member of the British Institute of Embalmers. In 1997 he was awarded a Master's Degree in Business Administration (MBA).

In the Belle Epoque of the 1890s Joseph Arthur Hey was born in 1867 in the Manningham area of Bradford. He left school at the age of 14 and worked as a wool sorter responsible for grading the daily intake of unwashed wool which arrived in the family owned mill at the junction of Thornton Road and City Road. Here he sorted the wool from hill and lowland sheep from home and the Antipodes according to its quality and the end product as carpeting or fine worsteds and broadcloth or for long lasting tweeds and serges.

When he was free from the demands of the mill he plied for hire outside the railway stations, with a horse drawn four-wheeler cab, borrowed from his undertaker father-in-law.

Left: Mr and Mrs Joseph A. Hey pictured towards the end of the 18th Century.
Top: Herbert Hey circa 1925 standing alongside what is believed to be their first motor hearse.

Married in 1892 aged 25 years, his wife Emily encouraged him to help and work within her father's business, in the census of 1901 he describes himself as a 'Cab Proprietor'/Undertaker; a foretaste of what was to come. On 3 October, 1908, he and his wife left his father in law's business and placed the company's first advert on page 2 in the Bradford Daily Argus. It read "Joseph Arthur Hey, Undertaker and Carriage Proprietor (late with W. Turnpenny). Funerals completely furnished. Personal attention day or night. Distance no object, Telephone 1892".

The Turnpenny undertaking dynasty traced its origins to Mr Watson Turnpenny, born in Bradford in 1838. In 1851, aged 13 years, he was described as a factory worker living in Clarence Street, Horton. A turn of the century advert declares that he started in business on his own account in 1856 – aged just 18 years. He was married in 1859 and Parish records show him as a Cabinet Maker and he moved with his new wife to Holbeck in Leeds and appeared on the census of 1861 as an undertaker – employer. In 1871, now living at 330, Manchester Road, Horton. His diversity of business and an eye for the opportunity is clear to see, he describes himself as undertaker, cabinet maker (the Master) and furniture dealer. On 7 November, 1871, he and two others applied for a patent for "improvements in looms for weaving".

He applied for another Patent on a trouser press on 22 February, 1918, aged 80 years. He died in 1925 aged 87 years.

Watson Turnpenny and his wife Elizabeth (the first of three wives, each of whom he would outlive) would have four daughters, Sarah, Martha, Emily and Mary. All four daughters would work in their father's business. Emily, listed in the 1891 census an 'Undertaker's Assistant', married Joseph Hey in 1892. Joseph would become but one of Watson Turnpenny's son-in-laws to join the family firm.

Sarah, born in 1860, married John North, a butcher in 1880 and they had three children, the eldest, Ellen, went on to become a book keeper, at an Undertakers in the census of 1901. Martha, Watson's second daughter, was born in 1862 and married John Coxon in 1885, initially described as a solicitors clerk in 1891, he appeared in the 1901 census as Solicitor's Cashier and by 1911 he was an Undertaker. The business of W. Turnpenny & Coxon would continue to advertise and trade until 1937 in Manningham Lane and Bingley.

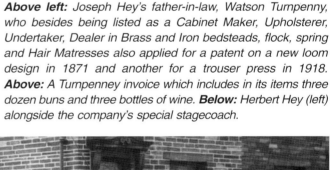

Above left: Joseph Hey's father-in-law, Watson Turnpenny, who besides being listed as a Cabinet Maker, Upholsterer, Undertaker, Dealer in Brass and Iron bedsteads, flock, spring and Hair Matresses also applied for a patent on a new loom design in 1871 and another for a trouser press in 1918. *Above:* A Turnpenney invoice which includes in its items three dozen buns and three bottles of wine. *Below:* Herbert Hey (left) alongside the company's special stagecoach.

FUNERAL OF MR. R. HANNAM

There was a large gathering of mourners at the funeral at Undercliffe Cemetery, Bradford, yesterday, of Mr R. J. Hannam, a well-known Bradford sportsman, and at one time a prominent racehorse and greyhound owner.

Watson Turnpenny's fourth daughter Mary was born in 1873 and married Herbert Fox in July 1895. Originally from Pocklington, their marriage brought him to Bradford and in 1901 he described himself as an Undertaker's Assistant. In May 1923, a funeral invoice shows him trading in his own right "Herbert E. Fox, Complete Funeral Undertaker".

Joseph Hey was built to be an undertaker: he was a tall imposing man who added an aura of his own to the black business uniform of knee length frock coat and a silk top hat. His life-long love of music enabled him to conduct his business with the desired regularity of organisation, dignity and sympathetic bearing which were balm to his bereaved customers. In his spare time he participated in the tuneful activities of the Little Horton Orpheous Glee Union Band, both as a member and as president.

But working for his father-in-law had its downside. Joseph clearly had ideas and ambitions of his own, something which perhaps did not sit well with the older man long used to ruling the family roost. In 1908 Joseph Hey with support from his wife, set up in business on his own. Evidence from the time suggests that the split may have been rather less than amicable.

Nevertheless, with a desire to uphold, or better, the standards of his father-in-law's company Joseph Hey, aided by his knowledgeable wife, practised his profession with all the pride of one who does a job well. His brochures declared a policy of keeping abreast of the times and what exciting times the early

Above: The funeral of Mr R Hannam, 1928, a well-know Bradford sportsman and a one-time greyhound and racehorse owner. Notice the horse made from flowers on top of the hearse. *Left:* The "Herbert E. Fox, Complete Funeral Undertaker" invoice from 1923. *Below:* A Joseph A. Hey & Son Rolls Royce 'Silver Wraith' hearse. The chasis was commissioned from the British Wagon Company Limited in 1949 with the body being constructed by Dotteridge Brothers of London at a cost of £2,360, around £60,000 today.

decades of the new century were now that the old Queen was dead and fashions and customs were changing in the modern world!

Joseph Hey and his family made available every possible facility to ease the troubles of those left behind by making the last journey of the deceased loved one as dignified and memorable as could be afforded.

At the turn of the century Bradford was far removed from the unhealthily dangerous place it had been in the first four decades of the 19th Century, though death was still a common visitor to the homes of families in all stations of life. Clean water was more readily available, especially in newer houses, and sewage disposal was much better organised, whilst medical science had made considerable advances during the Queen's long reign. Child death, however, was still frequent and consumption, or tuberculosis, were then incurable. The great outbreaks of cholera were past, but infections and diseases which we can cure today were still killers. Social conditions being what they were, those whose diet and accommodation were sub-standard died more frequently than others more fortunately placed.

To meet the regular cost of funerals many families saved with weekly payments to their local friendly societies in order to avoid the shame of having one's beloved buried in a pauper's grave. It is from these single-purpose friendly societies that many of today's mighty insurance companies and building societies have grown.

Today, those same high standards are maintained by the present family business, following in the traditions adhered to by Joseph's son, Herbert, and daughters, Florence Emily (Emmie) and Sarahannah, who developed the company in the second generation. It was their generation which took the revolutionary step of replacing horse-drawn hearses with motor cars in the 1920s, although horses were still kept for a time, for those who preferred the sheer magnificence of shiny black horses bedecked with sable feathers.

Above: *Joseph A. Hey & Son letterheads from 1933 (top) and 1951.* *Below:* *Herbert (right) and Arthur (left) Hey receiving a new fleet of Austin Princess Limousines in 1965.*

A Private Service Chapel was installed in 1930 next to a dignified Reception Room where mourners could meet without being stared at. Such a facility was then unique and the thoughtfulness was much appreciated by those who found a funeral gathering in the public rooms of a hotel exacerbated their ordeal to an unwanted level. The famous department store, Brown Muff, ran its own Funeral Director Services for the benefit of life-long clients who had furnished their homes and dressed their families under their hospitable roofs. When Brown Muff closed its funeral department the tasteful fittings were subsequently acquired by Joseph A. Hey & Son.

By the time Arthur Hey, the third generation of the Hey family who had worked alongside his father for many years, took over, the firm was one of the largest Funeral Directors in Yorkshire. Arthur went on to inherit, and keep up the Hey family's well-deserved reputation for service and dignity, always so important to those left behind. In the 1950s he bought the vacant premises at 468 and 470 Great Horton Road next to the existing premises which still contained the former stables. The entire block was redeveloped to provide under one roof the in-house facilities of a joiner's shop where coffins are made, as well as containing a mortuary and sufficient garaging for a fleet of vehicles.

The existing chapel was kept, whilst the comfortable reception room was enlarged and the rest rooms established.

Today, the chapel continues to provide a peaceful sanctuary in which a memorial service may be conducted. Hey's also provide quiet, dignified, Rest Rooms where the earthly remains of loved ones, which have been removed from homes or hospitals in advance of the funeral arrangements, can lie undisturbed and insulated from the hustle of modern life. These simple, tasteful rooms enable relatives and friends to commune with and pray for, the departed in total privacy.

Joseph A. Hey & Son Ltd is proud of its staff, not least of those who achieved their Diploma in Funeral Directing and those who qualify to become registered members of the British Institute of Embalmers, who caringly and skillfully prepare the deceased for their farewell and final journeys.

The visit to see a loved one can bring considerable relief to mourners who sees their relatives totally relaxed and at peace. It is a biological fact that the skin of the deceased loses the marks of age and discomfort, and the relative sees their loved one freed from all the worries or illness which may have marked their last years.

Hey family members still involved with the company are Joan (Jo) Hey Morphet, the Company Secretary, and Kathryn Hey. The company offers a funeral service second to none, even still providing horse drawn hearses on request! Apart from the latter, and the continuing quality and dignity, the modern funeral would appear very simple to the founders, accustomed as they were to the flamboyance of their times. As costs of personal services have risen Hey's has marched with the times in offering pre-paid installment plans. As dealing with a death in the family is complicated enough by the legal and official matters, Hey's also helps to reduce the worries by offering an all-in service which can include funeral teas to replace the traditional wake in the family home.

Top left: *Joseph A. Hey & Son Ltd's Book of Remembrance.* ***Left:*** *The Private Chapel.* ***Above:*** *The Reception Room where relatives and friends meet prior to a service.*

Honeycomb casket is formed using over 90% recycled materials, cardboard and paper, that provides a very strong, lightweight and environmentally friendly shell on which natural wooden veneers can be applied in the traditional way.

Innovation has continued with a patent for a new coffin cover granted in 2011, and another UK patent granted for an 'improvement to coffins' in 2012.

Today, from a funeral lasting several days in two cities, in three venues with thousands of mourners in attendance, like Jimmy Savile's, to the simplest dignified funeral, Joseph A. Hey & Son Ltd is able to meet every client's wishes. The years of experience and the knowledge gained extends to every aspect of bereavement including: repatriation to and from countries abroad, memorial headstones, exhumation and comprehensive advice on every detail relating to funerals. In an era when many family undertakers have sold out to large companies there remains a very welcome place for the personal touch that comes only from a privately run business such as Joseph A. Hey and Son Ltd, a member of the National Association of Funeral Directors.

In May 2004, the company developed and submitted a Patent Application on a remarkable award-winning economic and eco-friendly alternative to the traditional coffin. The dictionary describes a coffin as a 'box in which human remains are buried or cremated'. For anyone who needs to purchase one, a coffin is an emotional symbol of a close relative now-deceased.

For some families a coffin represents 'the way someone lived their life'; it might be the best casket that money can buy, or a very simple coffin. But for many others the coffin is only a necessary and unavoidable purchase that merely performs a practical function and 'it does not matter what it was made from if it's going to be cremated'. This point of view may also reflect the expressed wish of a relative before they passed away.

A Coffin Cover arrangement is a new and unique innovation in coffin design that combines all the necessary requirements of the traditional coffin with an enhanced visual appearance. What makes the Coffin Cover arrangement different is that it contains a separate internal coffin that is made of a simple biodegradable material that is removed from the outer Coffin Cover prior to the cremation or the burial taking place. The simple and practical internal coffin is the only item that a family needs to purchase for the funeral because the outer Coffin Cover can be re-used again and again. The internal coffin is very low cost to produce and the savings are passed on to the family.

Following on from the success of the Coffin Cover the company continued to innovate and develop the 'Honeycomb Coffin', and in May 2007, a further Patent Application was submitted. The Honeycomb range is now clearly established and look from the outside just like any other traditional burial or cremation coffin; what makes them unique is their construction. Instead of using Chipboard or MDF as the base material for the coffin, the

Joseph A. Hey and Son Ltd was established on 3 October, 1908, but the Hey family are very proud of Watson Turnpenny who takes their unbroken, family owned pedigree in funeral services back to 1856, which must surely be one of the longest established businesses in Bradford.

Top left: *Joan (Jo) Hey Morphet and husband Robert Morphet, pictured in 2007 with a Coffin Cover and the environmentally friendly coffin from inside.* **Left:** *A selection from the 'Honeycomb range' of coffins and caskets each made entirely of recycled paper and cardboard to make a strong lightweight environmentally friendly shell on which natural veneers can be attached.* **Below:** *Part of the Joseph A. Hey & Son Ltd fleet outside the firm's premises which comprises a complete funeral service under one roof.*

Crossley Evans
The Face of Recycling

Facilities at the company's eight acre Shipley site include railway sidings and two of its own locomotives, with access to all major mainline rail networks. The firm operates a public weighbridge, and amongst its other activities is a major buyer of metal. From small beginnings the firm has grown to enjoy an annual turnover of more than £20 million.

The story of recycling, however, goes back much further than a mere century. Indeed, recycling has been going on for all of human history. In times when resources were scarce archaeological studies of ancient waste dumps show there was significantly less household waste, such as ash, broken tools and pottery, being disposed of – with the obvious implication that more waste was being recycled in the absence of new material. There was even a philosophical and moral element to recycling, with advocates as far back as Plato in 400 BC championing the practice in Ancient Greece.

Long before the present day, there is ample evidence of scrap bronze and other metals being collected throughout Europe and melted down for perpetual reuse.

*Left: Tony Evans who took over the company in 1984 and wife Gail pictured on their wedding day in 1968. **Below and right:** Two views of the Crossley Evans site in 1979.*

Crossley Evans Ltd, with its head office at Station Buildings, Shipley, operates one of Britain's leading waste management and recycling facilities. The site has been in use for over a century, and is now supported by smaller satellite recycling sites in Halifax and Otley. The company specialises in the recovery and processing of recyclable materials, and is currently one of the top suppliers of UK based foundries. It also provides services to small businesses and domestic customers.

The firm is a family-owned and run business which prides itself on its friendly and efficient customer service. Staff strive to provide products and services that are of the highest quality possible. The company closely monitors the ever-developing range of legislation to ensure that it is meeting, and surpassing, its environmental responsibilities.

More recently, here in Britain dust and ash from wood and coal fires was collected by dustmen and recycled as a base material for use in brick making.

The incentive for these types of recycling was the simple economic advantage of obtaining recycled feedstock instead of acquiring fresh material - as well as a lack of publicly-funded waste removal in increasingly densely populated towns and cities.

And it was not just ash and metals. Back in 1813, Benjamin Law, in Batley, developed a process for turning wool rags into 'shoddy' and 'mungo'. These textile materials combined recycled fibres with virgin wool. As a result the West Yorkshire shoddy industry thrived and brought new prosperity to towns such as Batley and Dewsbury throughout the 19th century and well into the 20th.

Meanwhile, the industrial revolution created an insatiable demand for raw materials which is still with us today; ferrous scrap metals were particularly in demand as they were cheaper to acquire than was virgin iron ore.

The rise of the railways in particular created a heavy demand for metal, and throughout the 19th century the railway companies both bought and sold scrap metal in large quantities. In the following century the growing steel and car industries too created a new and ever increasing demand for scrap metal.

Today, in many third world countries millions of the poorest folk scratch a living collecting, sorting and selling the 'rubbish' disposed of by their better-off neighbours. In Victorian times in Britain things were little different for many of the poorest in society. Many people kept themselves alive by collecting, processing, and selling things being thrown away, searching waste dumps, scouring the streets or knocking on back doors, always on the look-out for discarded machinery, pots, pans, and other metal items as well as any other material which might have some small resale value.

By Edwardian times thousands of such scavengers roamed Britain's streets eking out a living by recycling materials for industrial use.

It was, of course, not just metals and rags that were recycled. Glass was good too.

Bottles were readily recycled, with a refundable deposit introduced by some drink manufacturers in Great Britain and Ireland as early as 1800, notably by Schweppes whose Swiss founder had set up business in London in 1792. Refundable deposits on beer bottles, pop bottles and the like would persist well into modern times, and be a source of extra pocket money for youngsters well into the second half of the 20th century.

Meanwhile, the advent of the Second World War had provided an extreme stimulus to recycling as shortages caused by the sinking of Allied shipping by German U-boats threatened to bring Britain's war effort to a grinding halt.

Massive government-promoted campaigns were carried out during the war, urging everyone to donate metals to the war effort, and to conserve fibre, as a matter of patriotic duty. In 1939, for example the Government launched its Paper Salvage programme to encourage the recycling of paper to help the war effort. Perhaps the most memorable of such schemes, however, was that to collect metal to help build warships and war planes. Mass collections of aluminium pots and pans were organised, with the metal recycled in the legendary Spitfire and Hurricane fighter planes. The legacy of this period remains with us today, not just in Bradford but throughout Britain: in the late Victorian period many thousands of terraced homes were built in Britain's booming cities, their front gardens enclosed by low walls topped by ornate iron railings. In Britain's hour of need almost all those railings were sawn off at the base and donated to the war effort: more than half a century later most of those railings have still not been replaced – a permanent reminder of recycling's finest hour.

In a more prosperous post-war Britain the street scavengers of an earlier age had all but disappeared. One, however, remained – the iconic Rag and Bone man with his horse and cart, and his famous, if incomprehensible, cry of 'Aaarghanooone', a cry much imitated by small boys.

In the 19th-century rag-and-bone men scavenged unwanted rags, bones as well as metal and other waste, from the localities where they operated. Henry Mayhew's 1851 report, 'London Labour and the London Poor', estimated that in London alone

between 800 and 1,000 'bone-grubbers and rag-gatherers' lived in lodging houses, garrets and ill-furnished rooms in the lowest neighbourhoods'. Rags and metal were obvious candidates for recycling. Bones, however, could also be sold on to be used as knife-handles, toys and ornaments, and also in the emerging chemical industry. The grease extracted from them was also useful for making soap.

A shortage of raw materials in the post war era of the late 1940s and 1950s led to a resurgence of the recycling industry, and with it came a golden age for the rag and bone man.

The handcart, or even just a simple sack, used of yore gave way to the pony and cart. Donkey stones, balloons, and even goldfish, were often given out in exchange for the items the rag and bone men collected.

A 1954 newspaper report claimed that some Rag and Bone men in the north could make as much as £25 a day collecting rags – a lot of money back then, though few made such a

handsome income. Four years later a newspaper reporter accompanied one rag and bone man, John Bibby, as he made his rounds through Chorlton and Stretford, near Manchester. For his day's load, which comprised rags, furs, shoes, scrap car parts, a settee and other furniture, he made a mere £2!

A decade later, however, the trade was in decline. Despite the BBC's popular comedy series Steptoe and Son of the 1960s, which helped maintain the rag and bone man's iconic status in British folklore, by the 1980s they were mostly gone. Rising scrap metal prices, however, would eventually prompt their return, although sadly most now drive trucks, not pony carts, and save their voices by announcing their presence by megaphone.

Facing page: A bird's eye view of the site in the1970s. ***Above:*** Tony alongside one of the company vehicles in the 1980s. ***Below:*** Pictured around 1981 is the Crossley Evans steam shunter on site moving rail wagons. The use of steam ceased in 1984.

And none seem to have donkey stones, balloons or goldfish to offer in exchange for the things they take away.

The renewed impetus for recycling had begun in the 1970s, due to rising energy costs. Recycling aluminium, for example, uses only 5% of the energy required by virgin production; glass, paper and metals too have less dramatic but very significant energy savings when recycled feedstock is used.

Energy costs were rising at a frightening rate as a result of world oil prices being pushed up dramatically by OPEC to create a worldwide crisis. But there was also a widespread fear of raw materials running out. The Club of Rome, an influential economic think tank, published an apocalyptic report predicting future shortages of almost every kind of raw material used by industry.

Meanwhile, in an echo of Plato more than 2,000 years earlier, ethical issues began to gain prominence with the rise of the environmental movement. Recycling paper, for example, saved trees; recycling metals saved both energy and the mineral resources still in the ground.

And apart from that, could we just continue to landfill waste willy-nilly forever and build larger and larger dumps?

What is the largest man made structure on Earth? Not the Great Pyramid of Cheops, nor the Great Wall of China. Incredibly, it is the Fresh Kills Landfill site in New York. Opened in 1947, at the peak of its operation, the contents of twenty barges – 13,000 tons of rubbish - were being added to the site every day. By 2001 the landfill site on Staten Island would eventually be 75 feet taller than the Statue of Liberty.

The rest of the world was heading the same way. And it had to stop before we ran out of space. Recycling has become the obvious answer. Happily, one firm was ready to meet the challenge: Crossley Evans Ltd, of Shipley.

Recycling has been carried on at the firm's site for over 100 years. The present firm was established as a limited company in 1942 by two brothers, Harry and Frank Crossley. In 1969, Tony Evans joined the firm bringing with him an invaluable set of engineering skills. Tony was able to introduce a number of large-scale hydraulic machines turning the company into a production

Over the years the company has moved from 'Rope' cranes with large masts which for many years made the site a landmark on the road between Bradford and Shipley. Today the landmark cranes have been replaced by modern hydraulic machines.

There are nine large cranes lifting tons of metal either with a huge steel claw or a magnet the size of a dozen manhole covers. Cars are dropped into cutting and crushing machines and pop out minutes later in rectangular metal cubes. In the old days, cars were simply crushed. These days, Matthew says liquids, glass and plastic are first taken out and tyres removed. Similarly, car batteries were simply mixed up with other scrap. Not any more.

Some 99% of material from the site is recycled and re-used in the UK – Crossley Evans is one of only a tiny number of companies in the country to operate in this way.

Crossley Evans runs a fleet of blue and green vehicles which collect from around the North of England. Yet energy saving, and thus care for the environment, extends to transport too. A rail siding allows 90% of material to be moved by rail. The company also runs its own two shunting locomotives (which have a loyal 'Train-enthusiast' following). On a good week, 22 wagon long trains shift over 1,000 tonnes of metal either to stainless steel smelters in Sheffield or steel, iron and cast-iron smelters around the country.

and process driven organisation – no longer just a scrap yard, but now a fully-fledged recycler.

In 1983, the company rebranded itself, adopting both the Crossley and Evans names, and began pushing ever further into recycled materials. Tony bought the company in 1984.

Today, the company provides mainly commercial organisations with recycling services across a range of materials: metals, wood, cardboard, paper and glass.

Over a 30-year period the second generation of the Evans family - Daniel, Adam and Matthew - learned their skills within the company.

The company is now headed by father and son Tony and Matthew Evans, helped by an experienced team whose average length of service is well over 10 years, the majority of whom live in and around Shipley.

Today, the company provides recycling services to numerous local councils county-wide, and is able to offer innovative solutions for recycling to many industries including handling Waste Electrical Equipment (WEE).

Crossley Evans Ltd represents the cutting edge of two thousand years of recycling history, helping ensure that our planet's scarce resources are used more efficiently than ever before.

Facing page: Rope cranes loading on rail-dockside into Hydraulic Shear in the early 1980s. **Top:** *A 2012 arial of Crossley Evans site.* **Above:** *Tony and Matthew Evans, 2012.*

Allan Jefferies
More Than Just Motorcycles

Allan Jefferies is a name synonymous with motorcycles not just around Bradford but throughout the world. The family firm of Allan Jefferies (Shipley) Ltd, today based in Berry Drive, Baildon, continues to maintain a tradition and a reputation forged over generations.

The foundations of the family firm were laid over a century ago. Joseph Jefferies, left with a peg leg as the result of a football accident, was a picture-framer by trade and a pioneer motorist who was quick to see a future for the horseless carriage. In 1901, he entered into an arrangement with some like-minded friends to form the Ross Motor and Cycle Company based in Shipley's old steam tram shed near the Ross Hotel.

The partnership, however, floundered, and old Jo broke away and started his own operation just down the road, selling cars, motorcycles and bicycles.

During the First World War, the 'company car', a de Dion Bouton, was used as a stretcher bearer for wounded soldiers from Shipley station to Saltaire hospital, allowing Jo Jefferies to obtain petrol (then a very scarce commodity) for the duration of the war.

Joseph's son Allan - another larger than life character - was born in 1905. The business moved to premises in Saltaire Road, Shipley, in 1917, where it was to remain for more than 80 years.

In 1928, the International Six Days Trial was based in Harrogate. Allan entered on a works Scott, which were manufactured in Shipley, and riding for Team Great Britain, won a gold medal, his first of six.

In 1932 Allan won the Scott Trial on a Scott, the first man to be best on observation and to set fastest time. This success raised him from notable rider to star all-rounder. Most competition riders were all-rounder's in those days, but Jefferies more than

Above: Pioneer, Jo Jefferies, who laid the foundations of the family firm over a century ago. Below: An early view of the Jefferies Saltaire Road premises.

Fastest in practice, he came in second to Geoff Duke on a Norton. His racing swan song was in August that year when he broke the Esholt Park track record.

All the while Allan's father, Joseph, remained active in the firm. During the Second World War, Joseph had kept the business afloat by repairing anything on wheels, even manufacturing wooden toys. The business was also helped by Allan's army captain's salary.

After the end of the war, the association with Triumph motorcycles continued to flourish, Triumph having built a brand new factory at Meriden, the previous one having been destroyed by German bombing.

By 1968, Jefferies was selling mainly Triumph, BSA, Honda and Lambretta bikes, together with Bond and Reliant three wheelers and Hillman cars. 'The Boss' was now the very active vice president of the Auto Cycle Union, chairman of the ACU's Benevolent Fund and a TT International Jury member. His brilliance as an after dinner speaker meant that he was in constant demand.

most, taking in hill climbs, trials, sand and road racing, and scrambles. By his mid-twenties he had broken a lot of bones - and a lot of records.

Allan won the Lancashire Grand National Scramble for Scott in 1933, but that year saw an even more important milestone in his life and in the history of the firm. At the Olympia Show, Allan signed for Triumph factory's Trials Team, with a road racing option. More than that, he took on the agency for the Coventry firm's machines. Triumph would become a name synonymous with Jefferies for decades.

Unlike many manufacturers, Triumph managed to keep afloat during the Depression. The Jefferies family firm was in a position to take advantage of the new range, which during Edward Turner's reign became the Tiger 70, 80 and 90, launched in April 1936.

Having gained a Gold Medal in the 1928 ISDT, Allan was selected for the 1934 British Vase 'B' ISDT Team and won Gold in Germany.

During the Second World War Allan became a civilian instructor to service despatch riders and then went into the Army, ending up as a REME captain in Germany post-war.

With most of his old trials pals retired, Allan decided to have another go at road racing. He entered the 1947 Clubman's TT on a Tiger 100, prepared in the Shipley workshop and finished second. He retired with a split petrol tank the next year, but in 1949, aged 44, he started favourite.

By this time though, there was already another member of the family dynasty, who would shortly be joining the long established Jefferies business, Allan's eldest son – 'Tony' Jefferies.

Anthony Jefferies was born in 1948. He left school in 1966 to take up a BSA Group apprenticeship, spending the first six months at Small Heath, Birmingham. Really a Triumph man, he then went to work at Triumph, finishing his apprenticeship in the service and experimental departments.

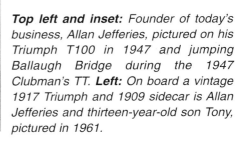

Top left and inset: Founder of today's business, Allan Jefferies, pictured on his Triumph T100 in 1947 and jumping Ballaugh Bridge during the 1947 Clubman's TT. **Left:** *On board a vintage 1917 Triumph and 1909 sidecar is Allan Jefferies and thirteen-year-old son Tony, pictured in 1961.*

In 1970 he joined the family firm and was thrown in at the deep end. Honda, Yamaha and Suzuki franchises had now been added to the Jefferies operation; it now moved Reliants to separate premises, and got rid of the cars to concentrate on motorcycles.

Tony started road racing in 1968 on a Tiger 100 - a real nail taken in part exchange - with home-made frame and leading-link forks. Tony became a works Triumph rider in 1971, and again in 1972 and 1973, competing for team Great Britain in the Anglo American Transatlantic Match race series. He had a good year at the TT in 1971, winning the Junior and the F750, and placing second in the Production race.

Jefferies senior started to take a back seat when Tony got involved in the business. Motorcycle dealerships were now beginning to lose their traditional rider-agent image and outlook; it was time to look forward.

Tony's first major business decision was to take a BMW franchise in 1971. Allan wasn't too keen, but his son had no doubts about the move. They were from different generations,

their judgment from different perspectives. The firm was the first officially appointed BMW motorcycle dealership in the UK.

Nick Jefferies, Tony's younger brother by four years, went straight into the business from school in 1971. Nick followed in his father's wheel tracks as one of the great all-rounders. He began trials riding, on an ex-factory Tiger Cub, in 1968 and became a very successful trials rider and member of the British ISDT team.

In occasional road races each year, Nick gained a succession of Manx third places, and won the senior in 1983.

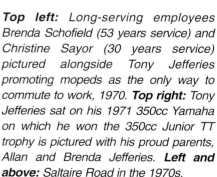

Top left: *Long-serving employees Brenda Schofield (53 years service) and Christine Sayor (30 years service) pictured alongside Tony Jefferies promoting mopeds as the only way to commute to work, 1970.* ***Top right:*** *Tony Jefferies sat on his 1971 350cc Yamaha on which he won the 350cc Junior TT trophy is pictured with his proud parents, Allan and Brenda Jefferies.* ***Left and above:*** *Saltaire Road in the 1970s.*

and the only man ever to win three TTs in three consecutive years, becoming one of Britain's top motorcycle racers on the national and international scene riding in world superbike, and grand prix championships.

At the beginning of 2003, Louise embarked on developing the existing BMW site by expansion, and embracing the new BMW corporate identity. This was a £300,000 project which involved doubling the size of the showroom and service department, and also introducing a 21st century approach to clothing and accessory display. Louise led the team through the development to completion in May 2003 resulting in the state-of-the-art facility from which Allan Jefferies operated until September 2010.

Above: The new Otley Road, Shipley, premises in 1996. Left: Nick Jefferies and John Hemmingway with his two sons Dan and Ben. Sponsored by Allan Jefferies they turned into two of the UK's top trials riders. Below: David Jefferies holds aloft the Senior TT trophy after winning his ninth TT title in 2002. (© Peacemaker)

With the exception of the MGP, he then concentrated on trials, with many excellent results. He gained a fistful of second places in the TT races including the elusive victory in the F1 race in 1993. Nick left the business to work on his own in 1996.

Allan Jefferies, an outstanding, if controversial, public speaker, died in 1978. His elder son, Tony, was cast in the same mould and has for many years spoken at club dinners and public functions.

In 1997 the Saltaire Road business was sold, and Allan Jefferies Motor Cycles, now solely BMW, was re-located to impressive modern premises on Otley Road, Shipley. Many of the long-serving employees moved with Tony, including service director Mick Lyon and company secretary Brenda Schofield - who has now been with the firm for over 50 years.

Meanwhile, at the end of 2000, Tony's daughter Louise, was appointed General Manager of Allan Jefferies Motorcycles. Louise had been involved with plc type companies in banking, travel and retail finance. She had always been a motorcycle enthusiast, as one would expect, and had held a full motorcycle licence since the age of 17. Her administration and sales skills were to prove an excellent asset to the company.

Tony now took a back seat in the company, being ever more involved with his son David's racing career which was going from strength to strength. As well as winning British Championship titles David became the first man to achieve the 125,126 and 127 mph lap speed at the Isle of Man TT circuit,

The company would have loved to have had a major re-launch, but tragically David Jefferies was killed in a high speed crash whilst practising in the 2003 IoM TT races. This was a terrific shock to the racing world, and to the Jefferies family; needless to say, as a mark of respect to David the proceedings at the shop were subdued.

Staff at Allan Jefferies were incredibly supportive, and carried on despite the difficult conditions. David Jefferies was everybody's friend, and it hurt everybody involved with the shop very much. In spite of the tragedy Allan Jefferies still managed to become the fourth largest BMW motorcycle dealer in the UK, and the largest dealer outside the M25 circle, something of which the firm is very proud.

By 2007 the showroom extension to 6,000sq feet had been completed. The shop was now full and had been complimented by customers from all over the UK and Europe on the high standards of display, cleanliness and atmosphere. The company now had a vastly experienced and enthusiastic team in place which took customer service standards to a new level. Allan Jefferies now has a total employee count of 18, a number unthinkable just a few years ago for a solus BMW motorcycle dealer. Allan Jefferies has made a major step forward with new computer systems and investment in equipment to cope with the modern technology and modern customer service standards.

During 2008 and 2009 it became increasingly difficult to cope with the volume of sales and service work, in the existing premises. There was no spare room for even a single bike. At the close of play each day the showroom was packed with demos, loan bikes, customer service bikes, with staff having to push 60-odd bikes in and out of the showroom every day.

The company had been looking for another suitable site for some time, and in the summer of 2009 was able to shake hands on a deal to buy some land just half a mile further along Otley Road. By November 2009, a brand new dealership had been designed and contractors engaged, with funding in place to start digging on 20 January, 2010, for a completion date on 4 September, 2010.

Newmason Properties, a building contractor that has done some remarkable work on mills in the Shipley area, started work on the new project. The staff had been shown an artist's impression of the new build and everyone was very excited about the new project.

Allan Jefferies wanted to create a dealership that would stand out as one of the best in Europe, with a total area of 14,000 sq ft. The firm wanted it to look special and have modern space for showing new and used bikes, clothing and accessories, a well-organised spacious parts department, and a service department with space and a clinical look befitting the BMW image. Needless to say, BMW Motorrad GB and BMW AG were right behind the new expansion programme.

After the initial infill of 60,000 tons had been deposited on the site to give the dealership the right elevation, foundations were in place by early March, with steelwork erected by the end of the month. The build proceeded on schedule and to the credit of Newmason Properties the firm moved in to start trading on 4 September, 2010. At a total cost of £1.7 million Allan Jefferies had invested not just in a new building but also in totally new computer equipment, new furniture, new display material, a new workshop and new diagnostic equipment. The company had created the best looking and most efficient BMW dealership in the UK.

The company's investment and expansion was shown to be fully justified after becoming the number one by volume agent for BMW motorcycles in the UK. Louise Jefferies had her efforts rewarded by being voted Bradford Woman in Business of the Year in 2012.

Top: A panoramic view of the Allan Jefferies showroom. **Facing page left:** Allan Jefferies' after-sales team. **Facing page bottom right:** At work in the servicing department. **Above:** Louise Jefferies receives the Bradford Woman in Business of the Year 2012 award. **Below:** An exterior view of Allan Jefferies' Otley Road premises in 2012.

Kirkgate for Shopping

People have been shopping in Bradford for hundreds of years. The earliest records go back to the 12th century, though no doubt there was buying and selling going on earlier still - despite William the Conqueror laying waste to the North in 1070.

During Queen Victoria's long reign, Bradford's heart was its bustling commercial centre swarming with shoppers. Since then the cityscape has changed dramatically, but though the city may have altered shops and shoppers remain a constant.

With over 70 shops and a market - all under cover - there's no better place to shop in Bradford than the Kirkgate Shopping Centre. A multi-million-pound refurbishment at the start of the 21st century created lighter and brighter malls and a striking central dome, specially lit by over 1,400 fibre-optic lights. At the heart of the Dome is Coffee Central, the ideal place to take a break during a visit. It's also where visitors found a striking new glass elevator making moving from one level to another easier than ever before.

Getting there couldn't be simpler. With 650 spaces, the Centre's car park, the second largest in the City, is the safest in Bradford and winner of the prestigious Parkmark Secure Car Park Award. Alternatively, The Centre is only a few minutes walk from Bradford Interchange rail and bus stations.

Built in 1976, the Centre was one of the original Arndale Centres. Since then it has since been refurbished twice - in 1988, and most recently in 2001.

Kirkgate Market goes back to 1251 when King Henry III granted to Edmund de Lacy 'that he and his heirs for ever shall have one market every week at his manor of Bradford'.

At first the weekly market, held every Thursday, was run under the auspices of the church, with the old Market Cross in the 'Westgate Box' as a long-standing reminder of that fact, alongside the very name 'Kirk' gate.

In the 18th century, Benjamin Rawson acquired the market rights and moved it from Westgate to Market House, Bank Street, bringing to an end the influence of the church – or almost. Sunday opening, would still have to wait another couple of hundred years – a reappearance of the Sunday markets held in Bradford in the 14th century.

The Bank Street site would, however, prove too small for the growing market. In 1824, there was a further move to Manor Hall, in Kirkgate, where the modern story really starts. At the start of the 19th century, Bradford was still a small rural market town of just 16,000 people, where wool spinning and cloth weaving was carried out in local cottages and farms. By the 1840s, however, there were 38 worsted mills in Bradford town and 70 in the borough. Some two-thirds of the country's wool production was processed in Bradford. By the 1850s, Bradford had become the wool capital of the world with a population of 100,000 and with the demand for shops and markets growing in proportion to the population.

Kirkgate market should have been welcomed by everyone. Yet when stalls were first set up around the once-fine Manor Hall there were a number of objections – reference being made at the time to 'a beggarly array of stalls and shambles', shambles being an old term for butchers premises and slaughterhouses.

Happily for posterity, the objectors met with little success, and the Kirkgate Market, originally called the Butter Market, has remained on the same site ever since.

A century later, in 1976, both phases of the then new Kirkgate Arndale Centre were complete. Shopping malls were added to make a complete shopping centre, which then remained almost unaltered for the next 12 years.

By 1988, however, refurbishment was necessary: work continued for almost a year, during which the centre still managed to remain open every single day. Once the changes, which had cost over £3.5 million, were complete the site, bounded by Kirkgate, Westgate, Darley Street and Godwin Street, was renamed the Kirkgate Shopping Centre.

Kirkgate Market and the car park were part of the building but belonged to Bradford City Council. The remainder of the centre was then owned by the Prudential Insurance Company Ltd. Early in 1987, Prudential Property Management had offered to undertake the refurbishment and produced new plans for the centre. The centre's tenants were consulted at every stage and their views taken into account. Each week a newsletter was sent to all units to keep occupiers abreast of work in progress. Four 'Kirkgate Reviews' were published to keep the public informed.

Left: Kirkgate Market in the 1950s. **Above and below:** *Interior views of the Kirkgate Shopping Centre in the 1990s (above) and 2012.*

New retail units, dubbed 'Gazebos', were introduced to bring in smaller individual retailers, as well as a Kiddie Ride carousel. An Information Bureau was added, staffed with the management's personnel who were issued with smart new uniforms of blazers and slacks in keeping with the new image.

The Centre had its two main entrances brought up to date and a new logo was introduced in 1997.

Three years later, in 2001, the centre was refurbished for a second time. A new feature dome was installed with its fibre optic lights, and a scenic lift was added, giving easy access between the two levels of the centre.

The car park had been acquired from the council in 2000; £1.5 million was then spent on improvements, providing parent and child spaces as well as more disabled parking spaces. Lighter and brighter, the car park would go on to win the Park Mark Secure Parking award every year as the safest city centre car park in Bradford.

Each Christmas the centre hosts the Bradford Junior Chamber Christmas Tree appeal which annually collects over 3,000 gifts for needy children in Bradford. Annual events, such as the Model Search and the Magical Reindeer Parade, are family favourites and have become a tradition. The Reindeer Parade heralds Santa's arrival at his grotto in the centre pulled on his sleigh by real live reindeer. Two young competition winners get to ride in the sleigh with him.

More recently, the centre has introduced a free gift wrap service at Christmas which has proved very popular. Shoppers who buy gifts in the centre can have them wrapped without any extra charge. Donations to the BRI Special Babycare unit from users of the service have raised over £1,600.

The 'Model Search' is a competition held each year. Winners in each category get the chance to be put on a modelling agency's books. Several winners have gone on to feature in advertising campaigns. The event is very popular with families and all the children love the chance to 'strut their stuff' on the catwalk.

Staff in the centre get involved in various community projects, such as St Mary's community gardens, where cash was provided to attract additional funding from other sources. As a result waste land was transformed into a well used and safe community garden.

A project with nine local schools produced teaching resources in the form of Big Books and educational films. The subjects were all about social responsibility and crime prevention with the aim of diverting young people from crime. Other local charity's supported include Bradford Food Bank and One in a Million.

Above: Kirkgate's Big Book project, 2007. **Bottom left:** *Free gift wrap offer for the festive season.* **Below:** *Kirkgate's Online Colouring Storybook.*

After being in the same ownership since 1987 the centre was sold twice in 2006 and is now in the ownership of Kirkgate Bradford Unit Trust.

The history of shopping in Bradford goes back more than 800 years. Today, the Kirkgate Shopping Centre is still adding its own chapter to that long story.

This page: *The hugely popular Kirkgate Lockin 4 Students where thousands of student took advantage of exclusive discounts.*

The centre is also doing its bit for the environment. Working to reduce its carbon footprint with assistance from Envirowise the centre's energy-saving measures include re-programming lights, switching off all unused appliances including printers and monitors, as well as water-saving devices in all the toilets throughout the centre. All cardboard, steel/aluminium and glass are recycled. All the organic waste from the juice bar goes to Yorkshire Water treatment works at Esholt where it is composted.

The first ever Kirkgate Lockin 4 Students on 2 October, 2012, was a hit with thousands of students taking advantage of exclusive discounts, giveaways and competitions. The whole event was promoted using social media. Even the rain didn't deter customers from queuing for bargains!

Today, the Kirkgate centre has over 13 million visitors each year. Meanwhile, retailers change as shopping trends change. Kirkgate has embraced social media with the use of Facebook and Twitter as well as its website www.kirkgate.co.uk....even Santa has gone digital with an interactive colouring competition on the centre's website!

Wright & Sons Ltd
Monuments of Memory

Memorialising a departed loved one in stone is a practice which has existed for millennia. Thousands of such monuments still exist from Roman times and earlier. And in Victorian Britain the practice reached new heights.

Wright & Sons Ltd has its origins in 1870, when the firm's founders are believed to have worked as 'banker masons' in the quarries in and around Bradford. The head office back then was at 179, Otley Road, adjacent to Undercliffe Cemetery.

Enterprising monumental masons would always endeavour to obtain premises as near to cemetery gates as possible. The firm of Frank Spencer, for example, actively canvassed departing mourners after funerals in the hope of obtaining trade, and undercutting the cemetery's in-house service. A short, sharp letter from the cemetery secretary eventually put a stop to the practice. Perhaps, unsurprisingly, the Spencer premises were taken over by Wright's.

A jewel in Bradford's historic crown, Undercliffe Cemetery opened its gates in 1854. It contains some 23,000 graves and holds a total of around 124,000 burials.

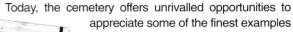

Today, the cemetery offers unrivalled opportunities to appreciate some of the finest examples of Victorian funerary art, all set within the original design of 26 acres of parkland. The cemetery also rewards visitors with its good vantage points and fine panoramic views across the city of Bradford and out over the Aire Valley. The site is on the crest of Undercliffe Hill overlooking the city and the townships of Eccleshill, Idle and Shipley.

The Bradford Cemetery Company was first registered in 1849.

By 1850, the businessmen who had established the company had agreed that the best site to locate their proposed new cemetery would be in the Undercliffe area on the outskirts of Bradford. A year later a hundred acres of the Undercliffe Estate was put up for auction. Five days before the auction in July 1851, however, thirteen well known non-conformist businessmen agreed to buy Lots 13 and 14, a total of some 26 acres.

*Above: A late Victorian Wright & Sons brochure. **Below:** Masons at work in the Wright & Sons Lidget Green Works yard.*

Amongst those signing the agreement were Henry Brown, Robert Milligan, Titus Salt, William Rand and Edward Ripley. It was, however, John Horsfall who actually bought the land for £3,400, the cost being divided equally between the thirteen subscribers.

Undercliffe Cemetery was to about to become a reality.

During the 19th century, many of the wealthy, influential Bradford families bought plots in the cemetery. These include many Mayors, not least the very first, Robert Milligan. In the centre, and along the main promenade, the family monuments are impressive, providing memorials to men such as Behrens, Bolden, Illingworth, Mawson - and Joseph Smith, the cemetery's land agent whose prominent 30 ft tall grey granite obelisk is today a listed building along with five other particularly magnificent memorials. With its laid out gardens, lawns, shrubbery and few graves the cemetery became popular for promenading in an age before Bradford had its first public park.

The partnership was redefined in 1891 when John W Wright left the business, leaving it in the hands of the remaining brothers Samuel and Henry Steel Wright. From then on the firm grew in line with Bradford's increasing population – inevitably matched by the proportionate increase in bereavements and the consequent demand for memorials.

Commissions also increased in value with the city's increasing wealth generated by the wool industry.

One of the most difficult commissions undertaken by the firm would be the erection of a 22 ton granite cross erected at Scholemoor Cemetery in memory of a serviceman who died in the First World War.

This page: *Early 20th century views of Wright & Sons Cemetery Works, in Necropolis Road (top), and Otley Road premises (left and below).*

Made from granite quarried at Crumb Quarry, the enormous stone was shipped to the famous New England Granite Works in Connecticut, in the USA, to be carved before being shipped to England to be installed by Wright's.

By the 1960s, with the increasingly popular practice of cremation, the demand for memorials had declined, and with that decline came a matching fall in the number of skilled monumental masons. Meanwhile, even restoration work on existing monuments declined due to the costs involved. In the mid-1970s Undercliffe Cemetery, one of Wright & Sons main sources of work, closed to new burials. During the first year it had opened 187 burials took place at Undercliffe. Between 1854 and 1928, 105,742 interments had taken place, including bodies transferred from the Parish Church and the Quaker Cemetery. The number of interments, however, actually began to decline there from 1900. By the late 1920s the number had fallen from a peak of 2,466 in 1898 to 696 in 1928. The decline in interments reflected the change in funeral customs, with ever more people opting for cremation. By

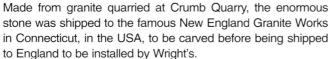

the 1960s, the Cemetery Company was experiencing increasing financial difficulties. Losses of the company were increasing; in 1976 the number of interments was just 72. Almost inevitably the Company went into liquidation. With no family heirs, and a business seemingly in decline, the Wright brothers, who still owned the family firm, sold the company to Joseph A. Hey & Son Ltd, Funeral Directors, in 1976. The funeral directors would, however, retain Wright & Sons Ltd as a separate corporate entity. That same year the late Herbert D Naylor, then the manager and registrar of Undercliffe Cemetery, came to work as the manager of Wright & Sons after Arthur Hey went to see Herbert at his home in the hope of securing his exceptional services. By the end of the year, however, there was just one order left on the firm's books. But Herbert Naylor and Joseph Hey's were not downhearted. With hard work and investment they began to build the firm up again. Before long the business began to grow and to develop.

Meanwhile, the kind of skills and 'trade secrets' that Herbert Naylor brought with him would prove invaluable – not least the knowledge of how to move huge pieces of stone safely. On one occasion whilst staff were puzzling over how to lower and then move an enormous slab of granite, Herbert laconically asked one

Top left: The erection of the 22 ton granite cross at Scholemoor Cemetery in the days before the introduction of hydraulic equipment when horses and chain power would be used for lifting such a large item. It was also the days before health and safety...note the missing rung on the ladder. *Top right: Examples of early Wright & Sons headstones, posts and kerbs. Above: A old company letterhead.*

worker to "go and buy four bags of sugar and when you return put the kettle on". He proceeded to pour four piles of sugar under where the slabs corners would sit and ordered the lowering of the granite onto the piles. When in situ, he began pouring boiling water on the corners, and, to the staff's amazement, as the sugar dissolved it rendered the slab almost magically easy to manoeuvre into place.

Acquisitions soon began to follow. In 1979 Redhead Brothers, based in Rooley Lane adjacent to Bowling Cemetery, was acquired; the following year the company I. Jennings & Sons, of Halifax was acquired. Most significantly the firm of W H Newton & Co, with a base outside Hunslet Cemetery in Leeds, and an office outside Harehills Cemetery was taken into the Wright's fold in 1997. The acquisition of W H Newton & Co, with its workshop and production facilities gave Wright's much needed additional spare capacity. Meanwhile, with memorials now arriving direct from India, new investment in machinery and training provided new opportunities for sales, not least through the internet.

The charity and its volunteers have undertaken work to educate the public about the importance of the Cemetery. Guides and newsletters, slide shows and open days have been held, as well as facilities and guidance for schools and colleges. Once again, the Cemetery is an asset to the city, and it continues in its original function as a fine place for a burial – and to admire some of the memorials produced by Wright & Sons Ltd.

The introduction of computer-aided design (CAD) now means that clients can have detailed 3D drawings of individual elaborate designs. Specialised memorial software enables inscriptions to be developed showing the exact font, size, style and design in full colour for families to check and approve before any work begins – printouts are vital when the inscription may be written in Ukrainian, Polish, Arabic, Urdu, Chinese, Hebrew and many other languages.

Left: Computer-aided design (CAD). Above: An early view of Wright's 'showground' at number 28 in the aptly named Necropolis Road, leading to Scholemoor Cemetery at Lidget Green, where the firm is still based today. Bottom: Wright & Sons Necropolis Road premises, 2012.

In memory of Herbert D Naylor.
A monumental mason and unique amongst men.

As for Bradford's famous Undercliffe Cemetery, a property developer acquired the site in 1980. Over the following years there was growing concern over the condition of the site. As a result the Friends of Undercliffe Cemetery was formed. Following considerable local pressure Bradford Metropolitan Council bought the site in 1984. The Council declared the cemetery a conservation area and sponsored a two-year Community Programme to begin restoration work.

A new Limited Liability Cemetery Company was formed in 1985, with council backing. The new company gained charitable status to become the Undercliffe Cemetery Charity. Since then, slowly and steadily, the number of visitors to the cemetery has grown.

Special thanks to Colin and Ann Clark and Reuben Davison for their contribution to the Wright & Sons story, and for allowing access to text and photographs from their publication 'In Loving Memory, The Story of Undercliffe Cemetery'.

For further information about Undercliffe Cemetery Charity contact: The Lodge, 127 Undercliffe Lane, BD3 0DW. Tel: 01274 642276.

Holmes, Mann & Co Ltd
The Whole Package

TELEPHONE BRADFORD 25212

BUSINESS ESTABLISHED 1890

Directors :
P. HOLMES
F. HOLMES
T. G. HOLMES

HOLMES, MANN & CO. LTD,
MANUFACTURERS OF ROLLING BOARDS, TIN, ZINC & WOOD CASES.

Speciality
3 PLY RETURNABLE CASES.

HARRIS STREET SAWMILLS
BRADFORD,
YORKS. BD1 5HZ

In the 21st century, Holmes, Mann & Co Ltd, based at Holman House, Harris Street, Bradford, is one of the best known names in the packaging industry.

The firm is a supplier to many industries, including light engineering, food, fabrics and plastics industries. It produces a large range of packaging products, with customers offered a 'one stop shop' solution to most of their packaging needs. The firm specialises in bespoke pallets, cases, combination packs, paper tubes, printed tape and packaging machinery. Although several local companies produce some items that overlap with those of Holmes Mann, none of them produce the whole range.

It was in the 19th century, in 1890, that partners Jonas Holmes and Matthew Mann moved into 202, Leeds Road, in Bradford, and founded the firm we know today.

Recognising the potential of the site they occupied, the partners would remain in business there for the next 40 years. The pair were experienced in the packing case trade and soon had orders flowing in from Bradford's then bustling wool industry.

Jonas Holmes, the great grandfather of the company's present Managing Director, was the son of John Jonas Holmes, a local journeyman case maker.

At the time the partnership was formed Jonas was 35 years old. According to the 1891 census he described himself as a sawmill machinist born in Hounsworth, Yorkshire. Curiously, in the census ten years earlier he had been working as a case maker and was described as being born in Toftshaw in Yorkshire.

On more certain ground, Jonas had previously been the foreman at a nearby firm of case makers before leaving to join what was at first the partnership of Holmes, Mann, Bennett, Bransfield and Cook, based in Bradford's Lower Ernest Street.

By the time the fledgling firm moved to Leeds Road in 1890 the partnership was down to just two members: Jonas Holmes and Matthew Mann. Possibly these were the only two partners who had got along with each other. Certainly the fact that they jointly owned a pony and trap

Top: *An early company letterhead.* ***Left:*** *Jonas Holmes (left) and Matthew Mann.*

suggests that they could work with each other without trouble. Or perhaps it was simply that with Jonas owning 4/7ths of the firm compared to his partner's 3/7ths that there was no room for argument.

Early on, the two partners decided to add rolling boards for cloth to their stock-in-trade and so became members of the Bradford Rolling Board and Packing Case Makers Society. This association had very strict rules which had to be read and understood because no-one was allowed to "plead ignorance in case of breach thereof". Members who lost their copy had to pay 3d for another one, a not inconsiderable sum in those days. The members' dues stood at 7d per week, and if arrears exceeded 8 shillings the man would be withdrawn from the shop. A member's contributions would also be refused if he did not bring along his card for them to be recorded. In those days the Society allowed no boy over 16 to be taken on unless he had worked in the trade before. The men worked a standard 50 hour week from 7am until 5.30 pm with half an hour for breakfast and an hour for dinner. In 1905, a new rule was introduced: One boy will be allowed to work at case making to every three men 20 years and over.

During the 1920s, Holmes Mann switched from using horses and carts to motorised vehicles. The stabling and hay storage areas used for the horses can still be seen at the factory. The new motor vehicles were well received by both drivers and customers alike, and were shown off at every opportunity, even if, with their manual starters, solid wooden seats, lack of doors, windows, heaters and radios, they were primitive by today's standards. Percy Holmes was once approached by one of the wagon drivers complaining bitterly of the cold and the lack of any form of heating in the wagons. Realising there was little he could do Percy tried to appease the driver with the

SPECIAL LIST, April 1st, 1913.
5% Discount.

MACHINE CASES		1" Planed, Tongued and Grooved	3d. per foot.
,, ,,		1" Rough, Unjointed	2¼d. ,,
,, ,,		1" For Shafting	2¾d. ,,
,, ,,		1½" Planed, Tongued and Grooved	3½d. ,,
,, ,,		1½" Rough	3½d. ,,
,, ,,		1¾" Planed, Tongued and Grooved	4½d. ,,
,, ,,		1¾" Rough	4½d. ,,
,, ,,		2" Planed, Tongued and Grooved	6½d. ,,
,, ,,		2" Rough	6d. ,,
YARN CASES		¾" Battened	2½d. ,,
,, ,,		1" Ends, ¾" Sides, Top and Bottom, and Battened	2½d. ,,
,, ,,		1" Battened	2½d. ,,
,, ,,		1" ,,	2¾d. ,,
¾" WOOD		4 Boards out of 3" Deal	
1" ,,		5 ,, ,, 3" ,,	
1" ,,		6 ,, ,, 3" ,,	

U.S.A. SHOOKS		3½d. per foot. 5% Discount Monthly.
MANCHESTER CASES		Made according to circular, and charged ⅛d. per foot off Bradford 1913 Price List.
SKELETON BOARDS		Mortised, Tenoned, Glued together and covered with Paper, 8/- per gross, on 1913 Bradford Price List.
DEAL CAMLET BOARDS		30½ × 15 × ½" full, 6½d. each.
,, ,,		30½ × 15 × 1" nominal, 7½d. each.
ROLLERS		1" Diam. 3½d. per inch per 100.
,,		1¼" ,, 4½d. ,, ,,
,,		1½" ,, 7½d. ,, ,,
,,		2" ,, 10½d. ,, ,,

Extra Wide Pattern Boards.

	½"	¾"	1"	½"			¼" 3-ply Veneer		22½ × 10	58/-
11	1/6	1/3½	1/1	1/- per grs. per in.			,, ,,		10½ × 11	29/-
12	1 8	1/5½	1/2½	1/1	,, ,,		,, ,,		30 × 10	41/-
13	1/10	1/8½	1/4½	1/4	,, ,,		,, ,,		30 × 12	49/-
14	2/1½	2/-	1/8½	1/6	,, ,,		,, ,,		32 × 10	43/6
							,, ,,		32 × 12	52/3
							,, ,,		30 × 15	61/6
							,, ,,		32 × 15	65/3
							,, ,,		28½/29 × 11	43/6

words 'Don't worry lad, it's only winter for half the year'!

In 1930 the business moved to Hammerton Street. There during the war years the firm took orders from the Munitions Supply Company to make boxes and grenade holders.

The firm remained a partnership for many decades until it was decided to turn the business into a limited company. The words Holmes, Mann & Co Ltd were painted on the chimney in anticipation of the event – though sadly Jonas Holmes died the day before the incorporation was due to take place. It would be Jonas' son Percy who would take the firm forward, together with his son Gordon.

In 1950, Percy and Gordon Holmes paid £4,000 to the Mann family for the use of their name in the new company, Holmes, Mann and Co Ltd. That same year the company opened its present site in Harris Street. The company's origin in a partnership is commemorated in the comma which still forms an integral part of the company's correct title.

Above: A Holmes Mann price list dating from 1913. Below: A 1970 delivery truck outside the company's Duncombe Way warehouse.

high, and had to be assembled on site around the gas separators before being given a police escort to the docks. Other more unusual commissions have included a 7-meters-long stepped pallet for shipping machinery abroad, and also a large packing case, with polyethylene foam lined drawers, hinges and returnable irons.

Other specialist packing commissions have included: several shipments of extraction equipment and ducting for Turkey, medical equipment bound for Yemen, computer equipment destined for China, a large power generator for Kuwait, electronic cabinets and switch gear for the Middle East, and industrial ovens for export to Texas

In the following years the company thrived. Such was demand for packaging that at one point the firm had as many as 120 employees.

Over the decades the old handsaws have long since been replaced by computer-controlled crosscut saws, and the latest packaging machinery such as case tapers and stretch wrappers are now supplied. Most recently, the firm has taken delivery of a state-of-the-art Printer Slotter machine from China, which massively increases throughput of corrugated cases.

In 2012, the firm delivered its first box especially designed to house Olympic torches. It was presented to John Skinner, who ran with the torch through Ripon on 19 June, 2012. It was made from 6mm plywood with hinges, latches and came complete with a bed of wood wool to cushion and support the torch.

Holmes Mann not only manufactures packaging, but can also pack large items of machinery for export on site. Recent unusual commissions include a multi-million pound industrial cleaning machine bound for China needing 19 large packing cases, as well as secure packing for high-value submarine hatches.

Above: A Holmes Mann service engineer's van from the 1990s. Right: The Holmes Mann Olympic torch box. Below: A complete packaging line in the Holmes Mann showroom.

The company has been set some interesting challenges over the years. In 1989, wooden packing cases with polystyrene fittings were made to transport portraits of HRH Prince Charles from Dean Clough in Halifax to London. Some years ago Holmes Mann manufactured a huge, and virtually flat, packing case for a metal gasket which was used by Red Adair to extinguish a North Sea oil rig fire. The largest packing case or crate within living memory was made to pack gas separators for Abu Dhabi. The crates were as large as many houses, 40 feet long and 14 feet

Holmes Mann remains an expert manufacturer of bespoke wooden packing cases, crates and pallets, designed to customers' specifications.

The company also provides related products such as frames, shelf decking, cradles and platforms. Holmes Mann can produce a broad range of corrugated cases spiral tubes and straight wound (convolute) tubes in-house. Holmes Mann also has its own printing facilities, enabling it to provide three-colour printed spiral wound tubes as well as in-house tape printing facility for printing self-adhesive packaging tapes. Using the latest core-cutting technology, very short tubes suitable for ribbons and tapes and many other applications can be produced. An extensive range of packaging materials is kept in stock.

Holmes Mann is also UK distributor for the Siat range of packaging machinery, which includes carton sealers, stretch-wrappers and carton erectors.

Meanwhile, with investment in modern machinery and technology, staff numbers have fallen to 42 – but those 42 have a collective experience of over six hundred man-years!

Today, with Paul and Simon representing the current generation of the Holmes family, the company looks forward to the future with a confidence born of more than century in business and a combined six centuries of expertise.

Top left: One of the company's stretch-wrapping machines. **Above:** *The old and the new - a photograph taken on the day the company changed to its new livery.* **Below:** *Paul Holmes (Managing Director) (left) and Stephen Rains (Company Secretary) (right) in the company boardroom with portraits of the family members behind them, 2012. Portraits from left, the founder Jonas Holmes, his son Percy, who worked at the company for nearly 70 years, and his son Gordon, who was the father to the current generation.*

Provident Finance
Simple, Manageable Money

Founded in 1880 by Joshua Kelley Waddilove, Provident Financial has been a part of Bradford's history ever since. Whilst many elements of the business have changed dramatically down the years, the fundamental principles have remained the same. Provident Financial is a consumer lending company particularly specialising in home credit - a system of responsible lending whereby local agents lend small, short-term, unsecured loans to people from all walks of life, delivering the cash to their homes and calling back every week to collect the repayments. This has been the main business ever since the very first days of Provident.

Provident's founder, Joshua Waddilove, was born in 1840 into a Puritan family and grew up with a strong sense of social duty and conscience. After attending Bradford Grammar School he went to work for an insurance firm, collecting money from house to house. It was in that job that he gained an insight into the needs of Bradford's working-class families.

By the time he was forty Joshua Waddilove had progressed within the insurance company and was able to support his family with money to spare.

He decided to use his spare cash to help feed and clothe struggling families, which he did by developing a system of issuing vouchers or 'checks'.

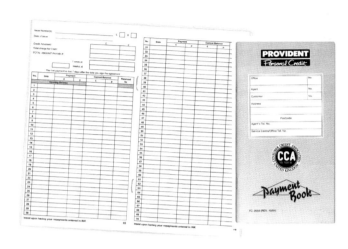

Top left: *A generous benefactor, Joshua Waddilove made significant contributions to Bradford Royal Infirmary, Red Cross and YMCA as well as giving his Bradford home to the blind and establishing the Waddilove Samaritan Home. Joshua also donated a significant amount to education in Africa and received a knighthood for his charity work.*
Above: *The relationship between agent and customer has always been at the heart of Provident and 127 years on, remains largely unchanged. For instance, customers still like the simple collection book showing exactly where they are with their payments.* **Left:** *After starting out in a tiny, first floor office, the scale of this building shows just how much the business had developed since its inception.*

In those days, he knew that if he gave cash to needy families the money might well be spent unwisely; alcoholism was a big problem during that period. So, he decided to give 'checks' to the neediest women which could be exchanged at certain local shops only for items such as coal, clothing and food. Word soon spread, but rather than be given 'checks' as charity, the women told Joshua they would prefer to take them as a loan and repay him in affordable instalments of just a few pence each week. This system fitted in very well with the self-help philosophy of the Victorian era, and soon became so popular that Joshua needed to employ agents to collect the repayments. Even better, Joshua was attracting so much business to the local stores that he was able to pay them a discounted rate to settle accounts. In a short space of time Joshua's unique form of economic aid had become a small business. He called his enterprise 'Provident', meaning frugal, economical, foreseeing.

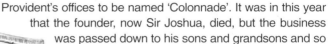

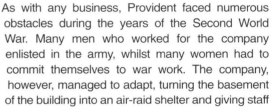

By 1910, the business had become the Provident Clothing and Supply Co. Ltd, with 85 branches nationwide, more than 3,000 agents and a yearly turnover of nearly £1,000,000. The company continued to expand, and by 1920 Provident moved to larger offices on a corner site in Westgate. This was the first of

Provident's offices to be named 'Colonnade'. It was in this year that the founder, now Sir Joshua, died, but the business was passed down to his sons and grandsons and so remained within the family.

As with any business, Provident faced numerous obstacles during the years of the Second World War. Many men who worked for the company enlisted in the army, whilst many women had to commit themselves to war work. The company, however, managed to adapt, turning the basement of the building into an air-raid shelter and giving staff additional responsibilities with roles such as fire wardens. Provident also contributed to the war effort by donating £50,000 to the Ministry of Aircraft Production, as well as buying a Spitfire for the Royal Air Force. The Spitfire, named Provident, served for 18 months before being used as an operational training aircraft. During the 1950s, things continued to improve for Provident. The company had regained some normality after the war years and the business grew steadily.

Provident joined the rest of Bradford and, indeed, the country in celebrating the coronation of Queen Elizabeth II in 1953. In 1955, however Provident held a party of its own, celebrating the seventy-fifth anniversary of the company. Employees from all over the United Kingdom attended a banquet held in Harrogate, hosted by Gordon Waddilove, Chief Executive, and Ernest Waddilove, Chairman.

The biggest change in the history of Provident came in 1962 as the company ceased being a private, family-business, and was floated on the London Stock Market, under the new name of Provident Financial plc.

Top: *'Provident', the Spitfire bought by the Provident Clothing and Supply Company in 1940 and a plaque commemorating the wartime gift.* *Left:* *An important part of the community, Provident's took an active part in coronation celebrations.*

Back in Bradford, four decades after moving into state of the art modern premises it was time to move once again. In 2010, some 700 head office staff moved into the new Southgate building on Thornton Road and out of their existing 1960s base at the Colonnade office block on Sunbridge Road. The 120,000 sq ft of offices in the £45m development was one of the biggest of its kind in the north of England. Meanwhile, Vanquis Bank had started trading in 2003 bringing the benefits of credit cards to people who often find themselves excluded by mainstream card issuers. Vanquis has since grown to become a successful credit card provider with around 800,000 customers in the UK, and has now started taking retail deposits.

Provident's expanding Vanquis Bank credit card call centre at its Thornton Road HQ is today but one example of Provident's continuous evolution, a process which has been on-going ever since its founding.

Whilst Gordon Waddilove remained at the helm, many changes were to follow. Shopping vouchers were introduced and people could have credit over a period of 50 or 100 weeks, rather than the 20 week limit that had previously stood. The Bradford skyline was also poised to change when plans were drawn up for a new, modern head office to be built on Sunbridge Road.

Meanwhile, in keeping with its founder's principles, being a model corporate citizen is a material issue for Provident. Having a positive impact on local communities is central to maintaining its 'licence to operate' whilst at the same time, providing sustainable benefits to communities.

In 1967, the new Colonnade opened its doors to Provident employees. As the contemporary design of the new head office suggested, Provident was keeping up with the modern world, not just in terms of architecture but also technology. In 1972, Provident installed a new computer centre, with a computer faster and more advanced than anything they had had in the past. There were just five main roles for the computer and it had to be manned at all times. The computer was extremely delicate and had to be kept in carefully controlled and monitored conditions. This meant that the air had to be conditioned and dust free, special suits had to be worn in the centre to limit the amount of dust brought in, and visitors could only see the centre through glass walls.

Top left: Staff from all over the country gathered in Harrogate to celebrate 75 years of Provident. *Below:* Frank Wood, who retired from the company in 2006 after 41 years of service, was one of the first employees to work in the new computer centre.

In the 1990s, the home credit service was launched overseas, and now operates in many countries worldwide. The strength of the UK and Ireland home credit business had led to international expansion, with Provident offering home credit as far afield as Central and Eastern Europe and Mexico. The success of that expansion led to Provident acquiring new premises in Leeds city centre from which to run the international side of the business. Following a demerger in 2007, the international business now trades independently as a separately listed company, International Personal Finance plc.

The vast majority of community involvement activities are now delivered through Provident's 'Good Neighbour' programme. Good Neighbour was established in 2009 and delivers activities in three ways:

• Local community project support – Provident identifies and support projects which address issues that are relevant to the needs of the community, for one or three years through its offices and employees across the country.
• Employee volunteering - Employees are encouraged to take part in a range of company-led volunteering initiatives.
• Employee matched-giving - Employees can apply for funding and volunteering grants to match the fundraising and volunteering activities they undertake outside work.

In addition, Vanquis Bank also runs its own 'Active Community Programme' which delivers activities at a local, national and international level.

At the international level, Vanquis works with the charity 'Teach Africa', which provides poor children in Nairobi, Kenya, with an opportunity to attend secondary school. Each year, five employees are selected to travel to Nairobi along with employees selected in previous years. There they help to administer the scholarship programme.

Today, more than 130 years since it was founded in Bradford, Provident Financial is a FTSE 250 company listed on the London Stock Exchange with over 2.6 million customers. The business is proud of its long association with the City, and to be a continuing part of the Bradford community.

Above: *The Provident head office in Warsaw, Poland.*
Below: *Provident Financial's new flagship head office on Thornton Road.*

On the move with Shipley Transport Services

It seemed like just another moment in the day-to-day life of Shipley Transport when father and son, Derrick and David Clarke, along with their trusty dog, set off to do an office removal to Kent. It was 1984 and this would be both a sad year for the Clarke family, but also a defining one for the business. Derrick suffered from angina and his elder son accompanied him on the journey to help with the driving and any associated heavy work entailed by the job itself. Dave, as he is usually known to everyone, took the wheel down to Canterbury and, having offloaded there, continued on to Connaught Street, just off Edgeware Road in London to deliver some expensive books to a prestige book shop. Just as Derrick was carrying in the last box, he collapsed and was taken to hospital, having suffered a heart attack. Sadly, he died shortly afterwards. This was an upsetting time for Dave and his younger brother, John, as they had also lost their mother just two years earlier.

Dave was determined to carry on the business that his father had founded and he took over the reins, even though he was just 20 at the time. Shipley Transport was still a fairly new enterprise in those days. It had been founded by Derrick and Dave in 1980. Born on 12 December, 1924, Derrick had served in the armed forces during the Second World War, seeing active service in North Africa. After being demobbed, his interest in motor vehicles saw him and his brother, Keith, getting involved in the taxi business. Derrick set up in Wrose, Shipley, and it was here that Derrick met Lesley Pauline Davis, his future wife. While in Keith's cab riding back home from the Bradford Royal infirmary, where she worked as a nurse, Lesley heard Derrick's voice on the radio. Having liked what she heard she enquired whose voice it was and the rest, as they say, is history. They married and had two sons.

Derek also worked as a driver/mechanic for Ogden's of Otley and Flower's of York, often taking Dave and John with him on his trips, thus sowing the seeds of his elder son's interest in trucks and haulage. Dave left school in 1980, aged 16, and had intended to join the police force, but the pull of starting a new business with his father was too strong. He joined up with him and never looked back. Based in Melbourne Street, Saltaire, hence the use of Shipley as a business name, the firm started off with just a Transit van, carrying out small jobs.

Top left: Founder Derrick Clarke scaling a palm tree whilst in Africa during the Second World War. *Left:* Lesley Clarke, wife of founder Derrick and mother of Dave and John. *Below:* With mum, brothers Dave and John are pictured on the bonnet of the family's Ford Zodiac in the late 1960s.

The Clarkes' reputation for reliability spread and soon one job led to another. Dave passed his ordinary driving test in 1981 and soon added a heavy goods licensce to his tally and was now well equipped to play a greater role in the everyday business of Shipley Transport Services. Larger vehicles, including a 7½ ton Ford D series and a brand new Bedford Tk were acquired, and the company was able to take on more and more work and operate further afield across the country. This period of expansion included the taking over of W&J Williams which helped the business go from strength to strength when Derrick suddenly passed away.

This was now make or break for a young man in his early twenties and with some support from his younger brother John, Dave put all his energies into making the company a continuing success story.

Despite difficult times in the latter 1980s, Shipley Transport was able to expand by renting larger storage premises in Idle, acquiring further lorries and, with the use of articulated transport, developing the business to include a wider range of haulage services for local companies.

By 1990 Dave was running the company single handedly when he met his present wife Joan (formerly Lowe) and they set up home together in Thackley with their children Christopher, James, Blair and Gemma. Joan was able to share the business work by becoming a co-director and taking over much of the administration side. A few years later Christina was

born. It was not an easy task in a small house, a lot of paperwork and five children, but the family flourished and so did the business as it continued to expand.

1995 was a difficult and a busy year for Joan, Dave and their young family. It saw them move their business to its present site at Dealburn Road, Low Moor, in July. They purchased 3 acres of land the year before and gained planning permission for a brand new warehouse to be built, which involved a lot of Joan and Dave's time being spent with architects, planners, builders and solicitors The family also moved to a much larger home in November of 1995, buying a 17th century farmhouse in Thornton. Sadly earlier in the year after a family holiday to Disneyland Paris at Easter and accompanied by Joan's parents, the family received the news that Joan's mum Christine had been diagnosed as having cancer. Sadly she passed away on 11 September, 1995. She had been a huge inspiration to Joan, Dave and the family and will be forever in their thoughts.

In 2000, a new office block and warehouse extension was built. Now there are some 35 vehicles and 45 trailers vehicles utilised on site, from a modest van right up to a mammoth 44-ton articulated lorry.

Top left: The former premises of W&J Williams, acquired by Shipley Transport Services in the 1980s. Above: Dave, Joan and their young family in the mid-1990s. Bottom left, left, and below: Construction of the new warehouse and further expansions in 2000.

It has been involved in some unusual jobs, including one at the old Salt's Mill. This involved moving a massive boardroom table and deploying a block and tackle to shift a huge safe. Although the face of the business has changed over the years, there is still some involvement with removals, as they continue to move people overseas to

Australia, New Zealand, the USA and Canada. Those entrusting their goods to him know that they will get a good service tailored to their individual needs. A full packing and unpacking service is supplied, insurance cover arranged, and all necessary documentation provided that is both flexible, accurate and guaranteed.

However, the main thrust now comes with arranging a reliable service for customers who want anything from a few pallets to many pallets of goods transported across Britain quickly and efficiently.

This might mean a lorry carrying a full load for a single customer or a combination of several smaller, part loads. The business is so well organised that a drop can be made in one town and a pick up made a few minutes later a short distance away. Consequently, vehicles are always on the move and seldom travel unladen. This keeps customer costs down and company profits at a healthy level, so everyone wins.

The Shipley Transport fleet in its distinct blue and yellow livery has always been keen to keep up to the latest technology including the most modern, high-spec trucks. The company has invested in new trailers with automatic lifting axles that lift when running empty or with a light load, thus saving on tyres. Dave has seen a huge growth in the use of Moffett mounted trucks; this is a truck mounted forklift and gives easier access to some more remote sites or those with an awkward terrain.

Top: Part of the Shipley Transport fleet outside the original premises. **Left:** A removal job for a family relocating from this house in Apperley Bridge (once owned by former James Bond actor, Roger Moore) to the south of Spain. **Below:** Grand finalist at the Peterborough Truck Show.

Shipley Transport combines a modern, forward looking business with that of a family firm.

As well as Dave and Joan at the helm, the third generation is now well involved. Blair, a keen horseman in his spare time, is the assistant transport manager, James oversees the warehouse and Christina works in both the transport office and accounts. The company continues to grow and over the next decade hopes to expand the fleet of vehicles further and possibly open another base in the south of England. One thing will not change, and that is a belief in providing a quality service.

All the vehicles benefit from onboard satellite positioning systems and customers can be fully informed as to the exact whereabouts of their goods at any given moment. Communication is important which is why Dave started using this technology way back in 1995.

As the managing director, Dave Clarke is the driving force behind the company. But, he is not a desk jockey as he believes in personal contact with customers who are friends as well as clients. This is a reminder of the days when he was building up Shipley Transport and meeting many interesting people.

Reliability is, perhaps, the single most important factor and is the main reason why there is such confidence in the company that the same customers return time after time. Why else would such major firms as Disposables UK Group continue to turn to Shipley Transport? Even so, it is not just the big names that have faith in it, but the smaller ones as well. They might only want a pallet or two moving, but they know that Dave Clarke's firm will deal with them with the same efficiency and respect as that offered to those with a much larger turnover.

Top left and below: Shipley Transport Services' 'Blue Mist" and 'Blue Thunder'. ***Above, left to right:*** *Blair, James, Joan, Dave and Christina, 2012.*

Sovereign Health Care
140 Years Caring for the People of Bradford

The Sovereign Plan enabled members to make provision in the event of illness. If a member had to take time off work or even give up their job because of illness or a hospital stay, the medical benefits fund would help to cover their everyday expenses. The Sovereign Plan attracted many new members.

Employers were now also encouraged to consider the Sovereign medical benefits fund for their employees. The Sovereign Plan was so popular that a 'his'n'hers' option was introduced with the slogan 'the easy way to join and pay'. This helped people in work to contribute through their employment on behalf of partners who were not employees.

In 1986 the Hospital Fund of Bradford officially changed its name to Sovereign Health Care.

With over 70,000 customers Sovereign continues to evolve its health care benefits today. A Sovereign Health Care cash plan now provides tax free cash towards a wide range of everyday health care

With origins in the 19th century, Sovereign Health Care, based at Royal Standard House, Manningham Lane, has been helping to make health care more affordable and accessible ever since. It is an independent, not-for-dividend company which exists solely for the benefit of its customers, business partners and the community.

Founded in 1873, the Hospital Fund of Bradford was created to raise funds for local hospitals which were then run as charities. By the 1930s the Hospital Fund was providing 40% of the income needed to run Bradford Royal Infirmary.

By 1933, the Fund began to evolve into the medical and hospital benefits schemes still familiar today. In return for regular weekly contributions, members received free medical treatment in some hospitals and convalescent homes. When the NHS was founded in 1948, the need for hospital benefits was reduced. Many hospital contribution funds closed; but the Hospital Fund of Bradford remained and moved with the times to provide a medical benefits fund.

In 1965, the Hospital Fund of Bradford developed the Shilling Scheme – the medical benefits or health care cash plan schemes which still exist. In its centenary year, 1973, the medical benefits paid out to members totalled £300,000 and by 1974 the Shilling Scheme became the Super Scheme. Most members transferred their contributions to this new scheme. Two years later the Sovereign Plan was born.

Top left: An early twentieth century view of the Theatre Royal, which once occupied the site of Sovereign Health Care's Manningham Lane premises. *Above:* Old and modern advertising of The Sovereign Plan. *Below:* A baby weighing competition fund-raising event at Low Moor Carnival in 1939.

related causes is of extreme importance to Sovereign, particularly those within the Bradford area. Not only is this where we are based, but where the majority of our customers come from."

To find out more about Sovereign Health Care visit www.sovereignhealthcare.co.uk

costs including dental treatment, glasses, contact lenses, prescription charges, physiotherapy, chiropody and acupuncture.

In 2007, Sovereign Health Care launched 'go-active', its first corporate-paid cash plan followed more recently by 'Asset' in 2011. Asset benefits employers and employees alike by paying employees tax free cash back towards the cost of staying fit and healthy. Employers benefit not only from a healthier workforce but also with help in meeting duty of care and other regulatory requirements.

Top left: Sovereign Health Care Chief Executive and trustee of Sovereign Health Care Charitable Trust, Russ Piper and surgeon Sanjai Addla with the da Vinci robot at Bradford Royal Infirmary. ***Below inset and above:*** Donating cheques to the BRI (inset) and Airdale NHS Trust (above). ***Below:*** Sovereign Health Care's Royal Standard House premises, 2012.

Sovereign Health Care is proud of its long history of charitable giving through the Sovereign Health Care Charitable Trust. As the company doesn't have shareholders, any surplus it makes is reinvested in the business or given by Gift Aid to the Charitable Trust. Since 1997 the Charitable Trust has donated in excess of £7 million to voluntary and charitable organisations.

Most grants are quite modest but the Charitable Trust is sometimes able to make more sizeable donations. For example, the Yorkshire Air Ambulance has received over £70,000 since 2009. The Sovereign Lecture Theatre at Bradford Royal Infirmary was opened in 2009, to which £500,000 was donated. The Charitable Trust regularly supports two local hospices, Marie Curie Bradford and Manorlands, as well as Bradford & Airedale Cancer Support. Most recently in 2012, £200,000 was donated to the Bradford Royal Infirmary Foundation Trust to part-fund the 'da Vinci' Surgical System, which offers a less invasive and much more effective alternative to open surgery for prostate cancer patients.

Russ Piper, trustee of the Charitable Trust and Chief Executive of Sovereign Health Care, explains: "Supporting local health-

Joseph H Clissold
A Century of Fine Clothmaking

Wool textiles have been processed, fabrics woven and cloth dyed around Bradford for hundreds of years. At the turn of the 19th century, however, Bradford was a small rural market town with a population of just 16,000 people, where wool spinning and cloth weaving was carried out on hand looms in local cottages and farms. All that was to change.

By 1841 there were 38 worsted mills in Bradford town, and some 70 in the borough. Two-thirds of England's wool production was being processed in Bradford. By the middle of the century Bradford had grown to become the wool capital of the world with a population of 100,000.

The number of mills stood at 350 in 1900. Many of these mills produced 'worsted', a fine wool fabric used in top quality clothing. The worsted industry made the district rich, and larger-than-life mill owners made fortunes. Bradford was nicknamed 'Worstedopolis'. Worsted refers to both a type of yarn, and the fabric produced using it. Worsted uses fleeces which have long fibres. In the processing of worsted yarn, combing machines make sure that the wool fibres lie parallel to each other and are of the same length. This produces a smooth, strong yarn and

fabrics that are hard-wearing and have a fine, smooth texture, whilst 'woollen' products are softer and warmer. Worsted yarn is used in clothing such as men's suits; woollen yarns are more suitable for knitwear and blankets.

Today, the Clissold Group, based at Oldgate Mill, Otley Road, Bradford, continues that fine tradition, as it has been doing for over a century. And despite a general decline in the textile industry it has bucked the trend, not simply surviving, but growing, to become one of the most prestigious names in the international textiles market.

Over the last 20 years the company has invested heavily in technology. The whole administration from fabric design to final despatch is controlled by an integrated computer system which adds efficiency of production to the craft skills of the workforce.

In 1910, Joseph Henry Clissold opened his cloth manufacturing business at Cleckheaton, near Bradford. The firm was later owned by Mrs Florence Hanson, who retired in 1975, passing the business to a consortium led by Adrian Berry.

Robert Laidlaw commenced spinning and weaving Scottish tweed fabrics in the north of Scotland in the 1940s, and became industry leaders in the application of colour in men's jacketing fabrics. The Laidlaw company joined the Clissold Group in 1989.

In 2000, the business was acquired by the Parkland Group, before three years later being bought back by the management team.

The Scotland-based Holland and Sherry Group, itself part of the larger USA-based Tom James Group, bought the Clissold Group in 2007.

Clissold's celebrated its centenary in 2010 by producing collections from the Joseph H Clissold archive, new cloths using designs from each decade from 1910 to 2010.

The Group's success and reputation is built on mixing the old with the new. Traditional craft skills work side by side with leading-edge technology at its Yorkshire facility.

Pattern weavers use the latest technology to bring life to the designer's creations. In bulk-production robotic warping mills and automatic looming machines cut weaving down times to a minimum. Investment in the latest loom models give the flexibility to accommodate large or short runs on a wide range of fabric types. Electronic jaquards give the clearest and cleanest woven selvedges. Clissold work closely with W T Johnson for the majority of their finishing processes. They use the most modern and sophisticated wet and dry finishing equipment, taking water from deep under the Pennine hills to help create a superb finish to its cloth.

British cloth is recognised around the world as the finest available. Clissold Group fabric has 'Made in England' woven into the selvedge. This, and the Clissold company seal, ensure the buyer is receiving the genuine article.

Today, after a century in business the Clissold Group is worldwide, with major customers not only in the UK but also in Europe, Latin America, the USA, Canada, the Middle East, South East Asia, China, Korea and Japan.

Top, facing page: Founder, Joseph Henry Clissold (left) and son Leslie Clissold (right). **Bottom left, facing page:** Mrs Florence Hanson. **Bottom right, facing page:** Robert Laidlaw, founder of Robert Laidlaw & Sons Ltd. **Top left, top right and inset:** At work on the Automatic Looming Machine (top left), Batch Decatizer (top right) and Computer Controlled Sample Weaving machine (inset). **Above:** The sign of quality, Clissold seal and label. **Below:** Oldgate Mill, 2012.

Trevor Iles - Keeping it Clean

Mindful of the title of this book 'Nostalgic Memories of Bradford', Trevor Iles Ltd, a forty-year-old company, has only a recent history and it is perhaps more relevant in the first instance to talk about its beginnings, it's 'pre-history'.

Many will remember W.P. Butterfield, the large engineering works in Baildon, employing some 1,000 people, which now unfortunately no longer exists. But it was from Butterfields that the founder members of Trevor Iles Ltd were drawn. The announcement of the route of the Aire Valley motorway going through the site of the Low Well Works prompted Trevor, who was the General Manager at the time, to start his own business in which he was joined by Jack Lumley, now deceased, and Kevin Dixon.

Most readers will be aware that the Aire Valley motorway has still not yet been built. Nevertheless, Trevor Iles Ltd was established, their first premises in Burley-in-Wharfedale and then to Valley Mills, in Bradford, to be closer to some of their suppliers and customers.

In the early years, the fabrication of waste containers was the prime function of the company. Following the introduction of paper sacks for waste collection, an early alliance with Bowater Scott confirmed the company's status. Acquiring a major shareholding in a blow moulding company for the production of plastic bins for council authorities further enhanced the company's involvement in the waste container industry which still continues today.

The alliance with Bowater Scott led to other paper products being introduced to the Trevor Iles portfolio and resulted in the emergence of the major hygiene and cleaning distributor we see today.

Since these early developments the company has been committed to offering high quality products and services, supporting the product offering with highly trained, specialist and informed staff in all areas of the company's operation. Clients include commerce, industry, local authorities, industrial cleaners and major retail operations. Not least are those national and international businesses whose standards are set globally: standards which Trevor Iles is proud to meet.

Further growth has been achieved by the acquisition of similar businesses in Sheffield in 1977 and more recently the 150-year-old Thomas Owen in Newcastle formerly a ships chandler.

The company's catalogue forms a who's who of famous and design-protected products which helped establish its name nationally, including a range of litter bins and hygiene waste bins for hospital and food industry use.

*Top: Part of the Trevor Iles fleet outside the company's Valley Road premises. **Left and above:** The company's Valley Collection (left) and Knight heavy duty litterbin (above) which was one of Trevor Iles key products in the early days.*

Despite the present economic situation the company are optimistic for the future having confidence in their market offering, their dedicated and professional staff and hopeful for the continued support of their loyal customers. The introduction of a new web site, a still a growing but successful work in progress has been welcomed by many customers who see it as an additional and convenient way to do business.

The Bradford head office is the main administration and manufacturing centre for the group's range of products and also controls the distribution and sales of the range of cleaning and hygiene, catering, floorcare equipment and service engineering capabilities. Today, the group's combined distribution capabilities mean it can service customers from Nottingham to the Scottish Borders.

Trevor Iles is a Director of Nationwide Hygiene Supplies, past Chairman and President of the British Cleaning Council, a former Chairman and Vice President of the Cleaning & Hygiene Suppliers' Association and an elected Fellow of the British Institute of Cleaning Science.

In excess of 10,000 separate lines are held in stock.

Thanks to the dedication of its founders, and the commitment and loyalty of its staff the business has grown significantly over the years. Today there are 80 staff working for the group.

The Iles group is also a founder member and shareholder in Nationwide Hygiene Supplies Ltd, a national organisation owned by independent distributors and run from an administration centre in Chesterfield. Nationwide Hygiene and its members are dedicated to providing local hands-on customer service to local, national and international customers.

The current organisation of which Trevor is Chairman has Kevin Dixon as Managing Director, sons Rob and Graham as Sales Operation Directors and daughter-in-law Claire as Company Accountant. Stewart Cawthraw, a long-serving employee, is also a company Director.

To all Trevor Iles Limited customers past and present, thank you for your support.

Top left: A view inside the Trevor Iles Sheffield depot. *Left:* An interior view of Trevor Iles Ltd's Valley Road showroom. *Below:* The Board of Directors, 2012, from left to right: Graham Iles - Waste Systems and Floorcare Sales Director, Stewart Cawthraw - Works Director, Trevor Iles - Chairman, Kevin Dixon - Managing Director and Robert Iles - Sales Director.

Flexitallic
Sealing a Reputation

Who would believe tucked away in Cleckheaton is a company, responsible for the invention of the spiral wound gasket which became the basis for a leading global business operating across 30 countries, inventing, engineering and supplying products which the world's major oil and gas, power generation and chemical process companies rely on to seal their millions of miles of pipelines?

From tiny tap-washer size gaskets through to gaskets the diameter of the factory wall, which are specially engineered with a massive range of components, combined to safely transport vast ranges of liquids, gasses and chemicals through the lowest cryogenic temperatures, to 1000°C across extreme environments such as the corrosive North Sea, all withstanding huge pressure variations.

Now The Flexitallic Group, The Flexitallic Gasket Company was formed in 1912 in Camden, New Jersey, in the USA by a German immigrant named Henry Bohmer. Driven by the industry's need for an improved, safe, effective sealing solution, Bohmer invented the 'spiral wound gasket' which did not need as much compression as other types of seal.

Spiral-wound gaskets comprise of a mix of metallic and filler material. This results in alternating layers of filler and metal. The filler material in these gaskets acts as the sealing element, with the metal providing structural support.

In 1941, Henry Bohmer died, and the business passed over to his widow, Mrs Ebba Bohmer.

Flexitallic's reputation and growth was established during the 1940s when Admiral 'Bull' Halsey of the United States Navy recalled his fleet and had six battleships overhauled and fitted with Flexitallic gaskets to prevent the steam loss that had limited their power in heavy seas.

In 1959, the Flexitallic Gasket Company was sold to a Mr Bradway, who would run the company for a short period until its subsequent acquisition by Manchester-based T&N plc.

High performance PTFE sheet materials were developed, and exfoliated graphite emerged in 1962. Towards the end of the 1960s the trend was moving towards non-

*Above: A copy of a Turner Brother (acquired by Flexitallic in 1994) letter which went down with the Titanic in 1912. **Below left and below:** Two views inside the factory in the 1960s. Note the sandals worn by the workers in the then not so health and safety conscious days.*

asbestos materials and Flexitallic was at the forefront of that movement with its non-asbestos fillers for spiral wound gaskets.

In 1970, the UK firm of Wood Brothers (Gaskets Limited) was also bought by T&N plc and the company was renamed Flexitallic UK Ltd.

Meanwhile, over in the USA, Flexitallic engineers working with inventor Lawrence L Guzick produced an energy-saving device in 1972 which replaced steam traps on US Navy ships, resulting in a saving of $10.5m.

Every other year, Chemical Processing magazine honours chemical industry innovations through the John C Vaaler Awards programme, and in 1976 this was presented by President Carter, on the White House Lawn, to Lawrence Guzick.

Flexitallic developed Sigma®, a biaxially orientated PTFE sheet gasket material for use in challenging chemical applications in 1982.

The company developed Thermiculite® during the early 1990s, initially for high temperature applications. Thermiculite® has since been established as the industry's problem solver for the most demanding applications. It would result in a second John C Vaaler Award.

In 1994, TBA Sealing Materials in Rochdale was also incorporated into the Flexitallic Group.

On April 22, 1997, the Texas-based Dan-Loc Corporation announced it had acquired the worldwide operations of Flexitallic from T&N. Dan-Loc Corporation and changed its name to The Flexitallic Group. However, Dan-Loc Bolt & Gasket Inc., which produces stud bolts and nuts, RTJ ring gaskets and flanges, continued operations under the Dan-Loc name as part of the group. Dan-Loc bought Flexitallic for $70 million.

Ten years later, in 2007, The Flexitallic Group was sold to OFI Private Equity (FDS Group), and in 2009 Eurazeo acquired The FDS Group.

The Flange Rescue Gasket (FRG) was launched in 2009– the first ever solution for sealing damaged flanges without the need for replacement or machining.

A year later the Academy of Joint Integrity was launched to raise awareness of sealing technology and to provide professional accredited training services for the industry, and to support its global client base.

Flexitallic has a proven history, from its invention of the spiral-wound gasket in 1912 to materials which have continuously pushed the threshold of chemical and heat resistance. In 2012, exactly 100 years after its foundation, Flexitallic launched a gasket which is better than any other gasket on the market, including its own - Change™.

So, next time you fill up your car think of the precision engineering required on every step of the journey, through millions of miles of pipeline, under the sea, across the land, through immense processing plants, all with specially designed, innovative sealing solutions, including Cleckheaton's very own Flexitallic gaskets, which have safely brought the petrol or diesel to you!

*Top left: Flexitallic's laser cutting service. **Centre:** The Flange Rescue Gasket (FRG), launched in 2009 (left). **Above:** The new 2012 Change™ gasket. **Below:** Chris Denton, Purchasing Manager of Cameron Leeds, has presented Flexitallic with a "Platinum Award", placing the manufacturer in the top 10% of Cameron Leeds' supply chain. Flexitallic is one of only eight suppliers, globally, of Cameron Leeds' 150 direct suppliers to currently hold Platinum award status.*

Rex Procter & Partners

75 Years Delivering Professional Solutions to the Property Industry

The first Bradford office opened in the 1950s at 123, Little Horton Lane; it moved to Blenwood Court, Low Moor, in 1995. The Bradford office opened primarily to work for the Bradford Technical College (now the University of Bradford) but staff soon found themselves working for other clients in the city.

Rex Procter & Partners has a longstanding relationship with Wm Morrison Supermarkets plc, providing Quantity Surveying services on the first new-build store at 4, Lane Ends. Ron Curry, who set up RP&P Bradford office, went on to become the Property Director at Morrisons, with Roger Owen joining the Morrisons property team after working at Rex Procter & Partners.

From the core services of Quantity Surveying and Cost Consultancy, the business has expanded to offer Project Management, Employer's Agent, Building Services Quantity Surveying and Contract Services. In 1984, RP&P Management Limited was launched, providing specialist services including Building Surveying, CDM Coordinator, Asbestos Services, Health & Safety Consultancy and Training.

Rex Procter & Partners has contributed to the growth of the City and built up strong relationships over the last 75 years, working with clients ranging in size from owner occupiers to national public limited companies including Wm Morrison Supermarkets plc, University of Bradford, Bradford Metropolitan District

Above left: *Founder, Rex Procter.* **Below:** *A montage of early Rex Procter & Partners documents.*

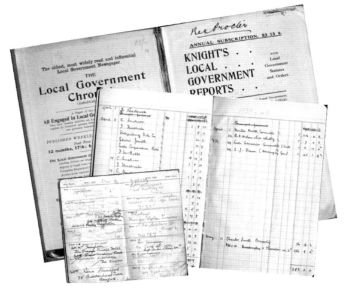

The well-known company Rex Procter & Partners is an independent construction consultancy. Rex Procter was born in 1904. He trained as an architect, and then a quantity surveyor - he reasoned that there were too many architects, and his chances of making good money were in doing something different!

In 1937, Rex established the business at 24 Queen Street, Leeds, initially as Rex Procter and Miller in partnership with Jack Miller. However, the pair disagreed on the direction of the firm; Rex wanted to be involved with bigger projects such as hospitals, factories, schools, and so broke from Jack who wanted to concentrate on housing. Rex moved to Blenheim Terrace and set up as Rex Procter & Partners in early 1940s.

Rex was an active member of the local community, as president of the Rotary Club, and Chairman of Leeds Rugby League. He was also a freeman of Kingston-upon-Hull - a hereditary title; Rex's forebears had been awarded the title following the Norman Conquest. Tragically, Rex was killed alongside his wife in a car crash in 1961, on his way to lecture to students in Cardiff.

Council, the National Media Museum, Bradford Grammar School and Yorkshire Building Society. Some 90% of work is through repeat clients – the firm believes in working in partnership with clients to add value to their projects and help to grow their business.

Notable Bradford developments the company has worked on include the National Provincial Building Society building, Centenary Square, Bradford & Bingley Head Office, Crossflatts, re-development of Valley Parade, the Atrium enclosure at the University of Bradford, the National Media Museum, the Rawson Quarter, Marie Curie Hospice, Number 1 The Interchange, Wm Morrison Supermarkets plc Head Office and Culture Fusion.

The firm became a private limited company in 2010. Over the years the company has built up its experience and client base to become one of the largest construction consultants and quantity surveying practices in the North of England, operating on a national basis from offices in Bradford, Leeds and London.

Strong client relationships and a high standard of professional service and innovation are embedded in the culture. What sets Rex Procter & Partners apart from competitors is a business model of senior level involvement on projects at all times and its high proportion of qualified staff. With an open, honest and approachable business style throughout the organisation, all staff are encouraged to contribute to the firm's success.

As an SME company operating nationally, RP&P is leading the way in community engagement and is heavily involved in assisting local schools in delivering home grown talent to the business community. Rex Procter and Partners is committed to being a responsible corporate citizen through a range of organisations and charities. Directors are heavily involved with local community organisations, fulfilling roles in the Chamber of Commerce (Chairman

Paul Mackie will be President in 2013), Bradford Property Forum and Bradford Society of Architects & Surveyors - former Senior Partner Geoff Emmett and Chairman Paul Mackie are former Presidents, whilst Director Joe Deegan will take on the role in 2013.

In 2012, the company celebrated 75 years delivering professional solutions to the property industry. The firm continues to invest in its community and is growing the business through new services – including RPP Energy Services Ltd launched in May 2012, offering Carbon Management advice and solutions to clients.

Top left and above: Recent RP&P projects, the Atrium enclosure at the University of Bradford (top left) and Centenary Square. **Below:** Some of the staff at Rex Procter & Partners Bradford office in 2012. Pictured front are Chairman Paul Mackie (middle) and Directors Chris Ing (left) and Joe Deegan (right).

Astonish
Cleaning Up Everywhere

Astonish House, off Staithgate Lane, Bradford, ought to be the cleanest premises in town – it's the home of the world-famous Astonish brand of cleaning products.

The firm, however, began life in most inauspicious circumstances.

In 1969, Alan Moss struck up an acquaintance with a sales demonstrator who was promoting a new ironing board cover in Woolworths. Over a meal in Glasgow the demonstrator asked if Alan Moss knew anything about a cleaning paste made in Leeds. Alan located the firm and obtained a few samples. The demonstrator was excited and suggested a joint business venture.

The demonstrator arranged a visit to Glasgow's largest department store where the manager placed a large order and allocated a prime location for demonstrations.

Alan drove back to Leeds, filled his small Anglia van with a stock of paste and on the following Monday arrived at the store only to find that his 'partner' was nowhere to be seen. He never did reappear.

Having spent all his money Alan had to soldier on. He went to a local scrap yard for an old oven top, rusty chrome and other items and began showing people what the product did.

To make the oven dirty Alan tried mixing gravy and water, but when dry it blew away. Undeterred Alan tried hard but the store manager was not satisfied. The whole venture seemed doomed until a lady dressed in a fur coat, bright lipstick, and obviously eccentric, came and left a card, telling Alan he really must contact her husband.

Thinking the lady was just odd, Alan carried on with sinking results, but two days later a larger than life character named 'Plymouth Joe' arrived at the stand asking why Alan had not called him.

Plymouth Joe then called another man known as Taffy, an experienced demonstrator, who came to the store and began demonstrating using far better 'props'. Sales rocketed, so much that after the two more days the store manager asked if the promotion could continue for another fortnight.

Within a few months many leading department stores, including Selfridges in London, were booked. Sales grew and grew.

Alan now had a thriving business when a bombshell dropped. The company producing the abrasive cleaning paste suddenly stopped

Top left: Founder, Alan Moss. Left: Alan and Trudy Moss welcome the Mayor & Mayoress to open the new premises in 1990. Centre: Astonish Oven & Cookware Cleaner. Top right: Astonish's new Shine & Sparkle range of products.

formulate new products: by the late 1990s the company had three chemists.

In 2000, new larger premises were bought in Pudsey. By now Alan had ventured into trade exhibitions in Germany, France, Italy, Spain, Czech Republic, Holland, Brazil, Uruguay, Paraguay, USA, China, Philippines, Taiwan, Singapore, Thailand and Japan. The end result was customers worldwide, many of whom have distributed Astonish for years. In some countries Astonish has become a household name.

making it. But by now Alan had better knowledge of cleaners, and wanted a less abrasive formula and one that was that was 100% eco-friendly. As a big animal lover too, he realised the importance of creating a cruelty-free product. A person who owned a product perfectly fitting the bill was contacted and bought out by Alan.

In June 2010, Astonish moved into a brand-new, purpose-built Head Office, manufacturing site, warehouse and distribution unit with a huge 60,000 sq ft. With a financial investment of some £5 million, the space should be enough to see Astonish through the next 10 years.

Alan's son, Howard now handles the day-to-day running of the business. Sales continue to grow - and no wonder when a Daily Mail consumer test in August 2012 found the Astonish Oven multi-cleaning paste to be by far the best product of its kind.

Now foreign customers began contacting Alan. In 1979 an American buyer ordered a large quantity of cleaning paste. The buyer was president of a large US appliance manufacturer who said that the paste was the best item he had ever used to clean cookware.

Unfortunately, the brand name, KLIN, could not be registered in the USA, so the importing company came up with a new name - 'Astonish'. Eventually the US customer agreed to accept an offer from Alan to buy the brand name from them.

By the early 1990s, the business still only supplied three items: cleaning paste, cleaning cream and stain remover bar. Meanwhile, the Astonish brand was gaining ever higher prominence, and by the mid-1990s a chemist was hired to

Top left: Alan Moss in 2012. **Above:** A selection of Astonish cleaners. **Right:** Howard Moss, CEO. **Below:** Astonish's new purpose-built head office in Staithgate Lane, Bradford.

ACW Garden Centre
Where Quality Counts

ACW is the oldest and best known garden centre in Bradford. And it's a place where quality counts. The firm was started as a part-time landscaping service in 1971 with capital of £40. Mick Walmsley and his wife Ann ran the business from their home in Baildon. At that time Mick was a senior Fire Officer based at Shipley. The business was registered in Ann's name: ACW was derived from her initials. The main reason for this was that firemen were not allowed to do part-time work, whereas helping one's wife, unpaid, fell into the same category as helping with the washing up at home.

By 1973, the business had prospered and employed 15 full time staff (plus several off-duty firemen), carrying out landscaping projects throughout West Yorkshire. A small nursery, 'Springfield Nurseries', was purchased in Springfield Road, Baildon, to house the vehicles and equipment. This was quickly out-grown and sold, and the company moved to Lowfold Nurseries, in Baildon, where it was possible to grow some shrubs and other plants, which were sold to landscape customers.

Mick then gave up his job in the fire service and devoted all of his time to the business: Ann took charge of the office.

In 1974, the first venture in retailing began by opening Bradford's first garden centre,

situated on a small plot of land between Busbys (Debenhams) main store, and their bedding store on Hallfield Road. The site is approximately where Fads and Halfords stores are situated on Manningham Lane opposite the Connought Rooms. The business remained there and was added to with the opening of a small garden and pet shop at 4 Chapel Lane, Bingley .

Top: The old frontage to the ACW yard. The white building on the left of the greenhouse is actually the old wagon body that acted as the shop and office in the early years. *Left:* Two aerial views from 1978 (inset) and 1985 clearly showing the growth made by ACW during that period. *Above and right:* Old machinery looking as good as new after a visit to the ACW workshop.

Since then, as the nursery has grown, Ann and Sally have spent more time at the Harden Nursery which now produces a large percentage of the plants sold at both sites.

On 18 July, 2000, ACW suffered a devastating fire at its Canal Road Garden Centre. The entire covered sales area, together with workshops, offices, staff rooms and store rooms were totally destroyed, leaving only the open yard stock surviving. Over the next nine months new buildings and layouts for the site were constructed whilst still trading from temporary buildings within the yard area. Good Friday 2001 saw the full reopening of the site. A modern garden centre for the 21st century had risen from the ashes.

Today, despite the current state of the economy, ACW are involved in a massive development at Woodbank to improve and increase their supply of goods grown in-house which will come on stream in early 2013.

The turning point came in 1977 when the present site on Canal Road was acquired. The derelict railway sidings, which were regularly occupied by travellers, were hidden behind a 7-feet high wall. In order to open the site it was financially necessary to close the Hallfield Road site, the Bingley shop, and Lowfield Nurseries at Baildon. The stock from all three sites was moved there to become the meagre beginnings of today's garden centre; initially a second hand wagon body was used as half shop and half office. The landscaping side of the company was closed to liquidate its assets, and those staff who wanted were re-employed by the garden centre.

Over the next few years the business continued to prosper. In 1982 a run-down light engineering works, Livetts, was acquired at Back Alton Grove, in Shipley. This was renamed ACW Engineering; it specialised in engineering and lawnmower repairs, thus the forerunner of the present lawnmower sales and service department was born.

In July of 1980, Andrew Walmsley, the present Managing Director, joined the company on leaving school - followed two years later by his sister Sally who is now Company Secretary of ACW's sister company in Harden.

In 1985, Woodbank Nurseries at Harden, near Bingley, was acquired. The semi-derelict nursery with adjacent fields totalled some 12 acres. The intention was to produce locally grown shrubs and plants to sell at both sites. In 1990, Mick moved to run the nursery leaving the rest of the family to run the Canal Road site.

The founding family is still actively concerned in the business, including the third generation in Christopher Corry who after studying at Askam Bryan College, joined the firm in 2008. The whole Walmsley family is always pleased to see that so many of their original customers and families still favour them with their support.

Top left: The devastation caused by the fire in 2000. Left: ACW's sister company, Woodbank Nurseries at Harden, near Bingley. Bottom: The new premises which opened in 2001. Above: The family, from left: Chris Corry, Mick Walmsley, Ann C Walmsley, Andrew Walmsley and Sally Corry.

Whaleys (Bradford) Ltd
A Fabric for All Seasons

Based at Harris Court, Great Horton, the firm of Whaleys (Bradford) Ltd makes no claim to be able to provide every possible fabric, but it certainly offers an enormous variety, from natural fabrics to specialist curtains and drapes. The company also has a wide variety of bags in its range, including coal bags, garden bags and textile bags.

In 1908, the business moved to India Mills, in Bolton Road, eventually moving to its present site, Harris Court Mills, in 1973.

During the first world war, weaving was suspended and silk-making abandoned. When normal work recommenced an industrial fabric section was established to furnish the textile finishing industry.

With real justification Whaleys can call itself a family firm: Harry Jowett, who took over the reins in 1900, was the great grandfather of the present Managing Director.

The firm was established in 1869 by Samuel Whaley. The original premises were off Leeds Road in Bradford. The activities at that time were silk and jute weaving, with one floor of his premises taken up with processing textile sacks and bags.

After Harry Jowett's death in 1921, the firm was taken over by his two sons-in-law, Fred Popplewell (MD) and James Robert McIlvenny. After the Second World War they were joined by James' sons Harry and James Fredrick, the latter being the current Chairman, assisted by his son and Managing Director, Peter J McIlvenny, who now represent the fourth generation of the family in the business.

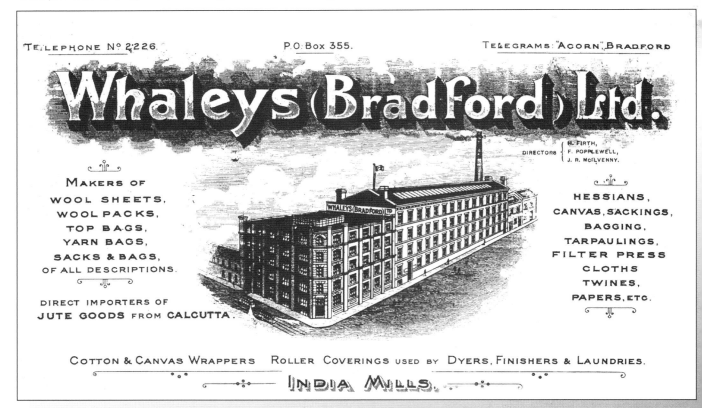

Nostalgic Memories
of
BRADFORD
PAGE AFTER PAGE OF PURE NOSTALGIA

In association with

AAGRAH
restaurants | event catering

STILL

ENGLISH

ESSAY
SKILLS
for
Higher and
Intermediate 2

WRITING
Critical Essay
Composition
Specialist Study

WRITING
Critical Essay
Composition
Specialist Study

WRITING
Critical Essay
Composition
Specialist Study

WRITING
Critical Essay
Composition
Specialist Study

WRITING
Critical Essay
Composition
Specialist Study

WRITING
Critical Essay
Composition
Specialist Study

WRITING
Critical Essay
Composition
Specialist Study

WRITING
Critical Essay
Composition
Specialist Study

WRITING
Critical Essay
Composition
Specialist Study

HIGHER

M.M. FIRTH
A.G. RALSTON

ROBERT GIBSON

ENGLISH

ESSAY SKILLS

for

Higher and

Intermediate 2

by the same Authors

KNOWLEDGE ABOUT LANGUAGE

LANGUAGE SKILLS FOR HIGHER ENGLISH

TEACHERS' MARKING SCHEMES

ROBERT GIBSON & SONS · Publisher

17 Fitzroy Place, Glasgow, G3 7SF, Scotland, U.K.

Tel: 0141 248 5674   Fax: 0141 221 8219

E.mail: Robert.GibsonSons@btinternet.com

ISBN 0 7169 8015 0

9 780716 980155

Pupil Books are at the core of the *Rapid Maths* course. Each maths topic is introduced very gradually, with a spiral progression helping to build confidence and ensure real success in numeracy.

Heinemann is part of

PEARSON

T 0845 630 22 22
F 0845 630 77 77
myorders@pearson.co
www.pearsonschools.co.u

ISBN 978-0-435912-34-

Rapid Maths is the 3rd edition of Number Connections

Heinemann

Today, fabrics continue to be a successful line, supplying mainly natural silks, cottons, wools. linens and specialist products.

A new range of eco-friendly fabrics, such as bamboo, banana fabric and organic cotton, have been introduced, whilst the firm also offers coated fabrics for digital printing.

Flame-proofed stage fabrics remain a staple of the firm, with continued expansion of the theatre drape manufacturing and supply side of the business. A new dedicated stage-fabric website gives full details of all stage fabrics and photos of projects completed. Coal bags remain a popular line, whilst, perhaps more surprisingly, so do textile bags for the wool industry.

Down the years the company has expanded and diversified, introducing a department which specialises in producing theatre curtains, along with a range of flameproof fabrics. In addition, a large fashion fabric section supplies fabric designers direct, with a separate mail order company. It is interesting to note that this included offering silk again, after an absence of 70 years!

A sewing factory manufactures all types of bags for the textile and coal industries. Currently, over half of the company's products are exported worldwide, particularly to North America and Europe.

Down the years Whaleys has seen a decline in the industrial fabric side of the business, especially sack and bag manufacture. By contrast the company has witnessed a dramatic expansion of the mail order side of its fabric business with online ordering now very popular. Harnessing modern technology the firm boasts a first-class website enabling customers across the globe instant access to information and on-line ordering. The company's computer systems have been thoroughly updated and renewed to cope with new technology. Significant strides have also been made in improving production and despatch, dramatically shortening the time between an order being placed and it being received by the customer, ensuring that Whaleys' reputation is not only maintained but enhanced.

Whaleys is a company that has seen many changes. The firm is confident of future growth and is now well placed to develop and service its markets both at home and overseas. Meanwhile the company continues to seek new and novel outlets for its products and is always ready to change to meet the needs of its customers in the 21st century.

Top, facing page: James McIlvenny (left) and Peter James (right) with the family founder, Harry Jowett in the picture behind. *Bottom, facing page:* A letterhead dating from 1920, showing the premises on Bolton Road. *Above:* A family picture comprising all the directors in 1997. *Below:* Whaleys (Bradford) Ltd's Harris Court premises, 2012.

Thermocable
Flexible Solutions

Founded in the 1960s, Thermocable (Flexible Elements) Limited, based in Pasture Lane, Bradford, has a quarter of a century of experience and expertise in the production of flexible heating cables used by electric blanket manufacturers worldwide. Thermocable also specialises in the manufacture of linear heat and water leak detection cables.

The business was founded in 1968 trading as Thermo Insulations (Yorkshire) Limited. The original site was Beck Mill, Clayton. In 1978 the company changed its name to Thermocable (Flexible Elements) Limited and, in 1980, moved to the current premises in Pasture Lane, Clayton.

Leslie Sykes founded the Company with just three employees. His previous job was as an electrical and refrigeration engineer. To begin with the new business focussed on the manufacture of anti-condensation heating cables used in commercial refrigeration. As the business became established other members of the family came on board. Michael Daniels, Leslie's brother-in-law, was in charge of Sales and Purchases; and Brian Sykes, Leslie's brother, was in charge of Production.

In the mid-1980s Thermocable was introduced to the possibility of manufacturing spirally-wound flexible heating cables used for heating electric blankets. Leslie designed equipment to deliver the performance required to achieve specific physical parameters for these new heating cables. As time went on the manufacture of flexible heating cables became the core business and Thermocable's capability and expertise associated with the innovation, design manufacture of these cables continued to grow.

Helen Sykes, Leslie's daughter, Andrew Sykes, Leslie's son, and Philip Wilkie, his cousin, all joined the firm in the late 1980s and early 1990s.

In the late 1990s, Thermocable began to export flexible heating cables to electric blanket manufacturers in Europe, South Africa and Hong Kong.

Thermocable acquired an additional facility at Hunters Park, Clayton, in 2001 to manage the increasing

Top: *Founder, Leslie Sykes (middle) and employees in the 1970s when trading as Thermo Insulations.* ***Left and above:*** *Staff happy at work in the early 1980s.*

detection/protection cables was developed which qualified to meet internationally approved standards.

Thermocable continues to work closely and co-operates with many of the world's leading manufacturers of electric blankets to improve safety, reliability and functionality of flexible heating products.

Although the world faces an uncertain economic future Thermocable has created an on-going opportunity through innovation to establish itself as a globally recognised and respected independent manufacturer and provider of linear detection/protection technologies.

demands being placed on the business, especially in anticipation of exporting heating cables to the USA.

As new markets were being established, however, it soon became clear that major difficulties were looming with the demise of manufacturing of electric blankets in the UK.

Andrew Rayner (Helen's husband and now acting-Managing Director) joined the business in 2002 tasked with the job of managing the complexities, threats and the opportunities associated with globalisation.

Realising that the manufacturing hub of electric blankets would soon migrate to China, Thermocable immediately started to investigate business opportunities in China. For a three year period an office was established in Shenzhen through co-operation with The China-British Business Council.

At the start of the millennium 80% of production had been sold into the domestic market. By 2012 over 80% of production was subject to export.

Back in 2004, Thermocable also began an intensive research and development programme to identify new cables that could be developed and manufactured from existing technologies in order to add greater value or penetrate new and more robust markets.

After a seven year development period a complete family of electric under floor heating products and a range of linear

Quality, dedication and co-operation are just a few of the attributes that Leslie instilled into the culture of Thermocable and these simple values have helped to establish strong commercial relationships across the world.

Leslie Sykes retired from operational duties in 1995, and as Chairman in 2008, but he has always remained available to offer his best advice to the current Board of Directors and to the Thermocable management team.

Top left and above: *Interior and exterior views of Thermocable's Pasture Lane premises, 2012.* ***Left:*** *From left to right: Mick Gatenby, Philip Wilkie, Andrew Rayner, Helen Rayner and Tom Robst.*

Paying Attention to Bradford Grammar School

'Hoc Age' is the Latin motto of Bradford Grammar School. A free translation renders its meaning as 'Pay Attention!' Certainly the school is well worth paying attention to.

October 2012 marked the 350th anniversary of the granting of a Royal Charter to the school by King Charles II.

Bradford Grammar School, including the Junior School, Senior School and Sixth Form, is a selective co-educational school which retains the best of the traditional grammar school ethos with a modern, forward-thinking approach.

Located on Keighley Road, a mile from the centre of Bradford, the school comprises of six main buildings on a 25-acre site.

The School has continued to grow in size, with the addition of the Kenneth Robinson Building in 1974, the Hockney Theatre and Sports Hall and the Clarkson Building, which included the Library and IT department, during the 1980s. More recently, during the Headship of Stephen Davidson, a new pavilion and swimming pool were added along with music auditorium and Sixth Form Centre. The Alan Jerome Building was operational from September 2010; in January 2011 it was connected to the main building, the refurbished KRB and Clarkson Building by the Learning Link. HRH The Duke of Kent officially opened the buildings in 2011.

Girls were admitted to the sixth form in 1984, and to all intakes from 1999. The school sets very high standards. It has long been one of the country's most distinguished schools and examination results are excellent.

Sports and games, too, are played to a very high standard. At the London 2012 Olympic Games former pupils Alistair and Jonny Brownlee were gold and bronze medallists respectively in the men's triathlon.

Exactly when the school began is something of a mystery: its early records have long been lost. Certainly the school existed in the mid-16th century. What is not in doubt is that Charles II granted the school another Charter, still preserved at the school.

The earliest school building was located in Church Bank.

*Top: The original Royal Charter granted by King Charles II in 1662 which can be seen on display at the School today. **Left, below left and below:** The original School building on Church Bank which was vacated in 1820 (left), the Manor Row School in 1830 (below left) and a late 19th century image of the new School in Hallfield Road (below).*

Tiny by today's standards, the school relocated to a larger building in Manor Row in 1820.

By 1861, the school had just 56 pupils; six years later numbers had doubled, and by 1875 had risen to 415.

Reorganisation led to a move to Hallfield Road in 1872.

Famous names such as musician Frederick Delius attended the school from 1874 to 1878, the Astronomer Royal Sir Frank Dyson was at the school from 1882 to 1886, and Sir Mortimer Wheeler, archaeologist, writer and broadcaster was a pupil between 1899 and 1905.

In the First World War, 1,150 Old Boys served in the forces. Poignantly, Ernest Sichel, an Old Boy of German background, designed the school war memorial unveiled in 1920 listing the 215 former scholars who would never return.

Clock House, a large 17th century house and its estate, was identified as a suitable location for a new school in 1919. However, building work would not begin until 1936. Old boy Denis Healey – Lord Healey of Riddlesden and subsequently Chancellor of the Exchequer - left in 1936 and did not see the new school completed, though others, such as painter David Hockney OM, CH, RA, would spend

most of their schooldays at the new buildings, whilst Olympic gold medal winner, the swimmer Adrian Moorhouse, who attended the school from 1972 to 1982, would never know the old school at all.

Remarkably, apart from teachers of 'Prep', there was no female teacher at the school until 1941 – Margaret Baker would remain on the staff until 1958, continuing to be the sole female teacher. There was none after her until 1976.

Work on the new school building progressed through the early part of the war, but it was taken over by the army. It was not until January 1949 that the building was officially opened by HRH the Duke of Edinburgh.

Since then Saturday morning school has been consigned to the history books along with school caps. Teaching too has changed: science has triumphed over the classics.

Today, the school has over 1,000 pupils. Under Headmaster Kevin Riley, appointed in 2012, the school continues to ensure that young people are fully prepared to 'pay attention'.

*Top left: The art room in 1912. **Left:** A 1949 view inside the former Jagger Library. **Above:** HRH The Duke of Edinburgh receives a gift from Bradford Grammar School after officially opening the new school in 1949. **Below:** A bird's eye view of Bradford Grammar School, 2012.*

Yorkshire Building Society
The Benefits are Mutual

Yorkshire Building Society, with its headquarters in Rooley Lane, Bradford, is one of the largest building societies in the UK. The Society is a 'mutual' organisation, owned by - and run for the benefit of - its members, and not outside shareholders.

Yorkshire House, on Rooley Lane, is a purpose-built development and home to more than 1,000 staff. The Yorkshire also has a second head office building on Filey Street. Many, however, will remember the Society's former head office, an eight-storey building on Westgate.

Yorkshire Building Society has grown to become the second-largest building society in the UK. The earliest roots of today's Society, however, can be traced back to Huddersfield.

It was in 1864 that the Huddersfield Equitable Permanent Benefit Building Society was established by three gentlemen who met each morning from 5am to 8am in a single room in the town. Early directors of the Society included a dentist, a shoemaker and a plumber. A 'permanent' Building Society was so-called to distinguish it from earlier building societies, which were wound up as soon as all its founder members were enabled to buy their own homes. Assets at the end of the first year totalled £4,044 13s 5d. There were six borrowers.

In 1866, the West Yorkshire Building Society was established at the Royal Hotel in Dewsbury with just two staff. Five years later it was doing so well that an umbrella and a rug were purchased for the office!

Bradford was slow to catch up, but in 1885 the Bradford Self Help Permanent Building Society was established in St. George's Hall Coffee Tavern, founded by Henry Bushell who, at the age of 24, became its first Secretary. Assets at the end of the first year totalled £185, with 43 members. During its first four years of business the Bradford Permanent opened for just an hour and a half once a week, but by 1893 the Society's office was fitted with an electric light. In 1915 the first lady employee joined the Society.

Top left: Founder, Henry Bushell. **Left and below:** *Early views of The Society's Queen Anne Chambers (left) and its Banking Hall (below).* **Above:** *Bradford Permanent Building Society pictured in the 1970s.*

By 1923, in Dewsbury, the staff of the West Yorkshire Building Society had doubled – to four. In Bradford, however, things were moving on more briskly: in 1930 the modernised offices of the Bradford Permanent opened at Queen Anne Chambers with rubber-covered floors and ultraviolet ray glass.

In the years following the end of the Second World War, many more ordinary folk decided to buy their homes. Yet, the day of the small, exclusively local, building society was over. In 1975 the Huddersfield and Bradford Building Societies merged. Seven years later the Huddersfield & Bradford and West Yorkshire Building Societies merged and Yorkshire Building Society was born.

Mergers continued when Yorkshire Building Society joined with the Haywards Heath Building Society in 1992. The Yorkshire also merged with the smaller Gainsborough Building Society. In the early 1990s, the Yorkshire became the first building society to publicly commit itself to not becoming a bank.

By 2001, Yorkshire Building Society had become the third largest mutual in Britain with assets of over £11 billion. By 2007 the Society had 1.8 million members and assets of £17.6 billion.

Today, the Society's community activity continues to be a key part of day to day life at the Yorkshire, with more than £4.7m donated by the Yorkshire Building Society Charitable Foundation since its creation in 1998. The year 2011 saw more than £462,000 donated by the Foundation to over 2,000 good causes, 90% of which were nominated by members of the Society. In addition, over 3,500 staff hours were donated as part of the Society's staff volunteering scheme – 'Actioneering'.

Yorkshire Building Society successfully merged with Barnsley Building Society in 2008, Chelsea Building Society in 2010, Norwich & Peterborough Building Society in 2011, and acquired the Egg mortgage and savings book and the Egg brand that same year.

'The Yorkshire' now has 227 branches and 95 agencies, with a further nine new branches planned to open. Assets have reached some £33 billion, there are now around 3,800 staff and over 3.3 million members.

One in four new mortgages is given to someone buying their first home. Chief Executive of the Society today is Chris Pilling.

Top left and below left: Opening of the new Bingley (top left) and Ilkley branches in 2011. Top right: Yorkshire Building Society launches a new savings account to raise money for the Yorkshire Air Ambulance. Above: Chris Pilling, Chief Executive. Below: The purpose-built YBS corporate headquarters.

Kashmir Crown Bakeries
A Bradford Jewel

Kashmir Crown Bakeries (KCB) was founded in 1968 and is widely acknowledged as one of the first Asian bakeries in Europe. Since then the business has grown from strength to strength with millions in revenue. The company currently specialises in Asian sweets, biscuits, cakes and savoury snacks which are famed throughout the world.

The man behind this phenomenal business is Mohammed Saleem, born in Bagh Sheri, Mirpur Azad Kashmir, in 1940. His father would have liked him to go to college but he knew that it was out of his reach. Instead he sat his Matriculation exams, and then got a job in a textile mill.

After working for a couple of years in the textile mill Saleem wanted to run his own business. "I had a deep desire to strike out on my own but I didn't have the means". This resulted in strong determination to set up his own business, though Saleem had little money.

In July 1961, Saleem arrived in Britain with only £5 in his pocket. He settled down in Bradford where he started working at the textile mill.

When he landed he had a determination to make a success of his life. After working hard for five year he rented a shop on Leeds Road called Kashmir Food Store supplying fruit and vegetables. He then continued working nights at the mill, and during the day he worked in his shop.

Due to the heavy workload, Saleem gave up his night job at the mill and began driving around the country delivering Asian sweets. This was a turning point in his life since he started producing Asian sweets. There was an opportunity for him to grow his business. He says: "I had £55 in total to my name." He bought an oven and a mixer and started producing Asian bakery products. A few months later Saleem received a letter from satisfied customer saying in short "What you produce is of outstanding quality".

Centre left: Founder, Mohammed Saleem. Left: Mohammed Saleem working in the textile mill in 1963. Top right: Mohammed Saleem in his first shop on Leeds Road Above: The first KCB shop in Carrington Street.

In 1970, Saleem bought a bakery in Carrington Street, Bradford, from Mr Whitehead. Saleem experimented making cake rusks, stumbling on the recipe for the best-selling, prize-winning, signature-product, the Crown Cake Rusk. It is still made to that original secret recipe and distributed throughout the world.

In 1974, a second shop was opened. In the first year he made £8,000. A third shop was opened in 1977 on Lillycroft Road, Bradford. Saleem believes that KCB's success stems from using traditional methods and recipes and ingredients of the highest quality.

In the new millennium Saleem, whilst remaining company Chairman, handed the running of the business over to the second generation. Expansion into Europe now became the keynote with distributors in Denmark, France, Germany, Italy, Netherlands, Norway and Spain, along with USA and Canada. Though known globally, the aim now is to make KCB a leading global food manufacturer as famous as Nestle and Coca Cola. KCB's Product Development Department aims to find new innovations - the next generation have a more westernised palette.

Chocolate is going to be a key ingredient for the future." However, whatever direction it takes, KCB will always be the Crown of all Bakeries.

Top left: *The prize-winning Crown Cake Rusk.* **Bottom:** *Mohammed Saleem pictured outside the company's head office in 2000.* **Top right** *KCB distributes internationally.* **Above:** *Part of the KCB fleet which distributes all over the UK.*

ACKNOWLEDGMENTS

The publishers would like to sincerely thank a number of individuals and organisations for

their help and contribution to this publication.

Bradford Central Library, Local Studies Department

David Busfield

Getty Images

Mirrorpix

A class at Woodend School in Shipley which conatained six sets of twins, 1914.